Joey Dunlop

a tribute

RAY KNIGHT

Published in 2000 by Mortons Motorcycle Media Ltd
Newspaper House, Morton Way, Horncastle, Lincolnshire LN9 6JR

British Library Cataloguing in Publication Data

A catalogue record for this book is available
from the British Library

ISBN: 0-9538357-1-5

Designed and printed by Redline Books

Contents

MICH

Preface

This book does not pretend to be a biography of the life and times of Joey Dunlop, OBE, MBE. Rather, it attempts to chronicle the career of the man who became a legend in racing history, particularly in the Isle of Man TT. Nevertheless, the research into his exploits over the years has produced a number of anecdotes that reveal a little of the character of the man, particularly his resourcefulness. My own 36 year racing career pales into insignificance compared to Joey's but it has enabled me to be a part of the racing arena where he has become so famous and to ride in many of his notable races.

In a very small way, I became a part of the Dunlop scene when Honda had entered Ron Haslam and Joey in the 1000k Endurance race at Donington in 1981. Being close to the competition shop at the time, Barry Symmons gave me the job of running the bike in. Sadly, it dropped a valve when they were a country mile in the lead.

Later, some many years in fact, I did another running-in job for Joey when John Harris had prepared a race engine for the CBR Joey was riding in the Island. Living close to John Harris at the time and, with the motor in my own chassis, the smoothness and top end power of the Scott-engineered motor, was a revelation. Delivering it to the island workshop made me feel a small part of the effort.

The final link in the chain of the genesis of this book came while working for the magazine, Motorcycle Sport, who wanted a diary of Joey's TT fortnight. In fact, it was Davy Wood who was the channel through which the information came; Joey was usually in the workshop or paddock and as a rider at the time myself, I knew better than to intrude. But it did set the idea running and from that day I started to collect contacts and anecdotes about Joey.

What of 'The Maun' himself? Born on the 25th February 1952 in the town of Ballymoney, Co. Antrim, Northern Ireland, William Joseph Dunlop OBE, MBE, has never been a public figure in the mould of modern media promoted sportsmen. Indeed, it was patently obvious as soon as the public spotlight became focused on him, that he preferred the light in his garage while fettling his own machines. His public acclaim was a puzzling fact of life to the man who would cheerfully serve you a pint across the counter of Joey's Bar, formerly the Railway Arms, of which he was Landlord from 1984.

After two visits to Buckingham Palace, in 1986 and 1996, 26 TT wins, five FI World Championships, as well as being voted as 'Man of the Year' by readers of MCN, Joey Dunlop was always a little diffident of his public acclaim. In a way that only another man from the Emerald Isle would recognise, he would rather have talked about almost any other subject than himself. 'I just ride a motorbike a bit quick,' is how he once responded to questions about the qualities that make him so special over the Mountain circuit. Clearly, it was something he took for granted. The roads of Ireland have been the anvil upon which many a road racing star has been forged. Irish motorcycle racing has bred a talented stream of riders that have graced the world's circuits from the days of Stanley Woods, Artie Bell, Alec Bennett and others too numerous to mention. In later years one could hardly fail to mention Philip McCallen and, brothers Robert and Jim Dunlop might well have gone on to far greater things if injuries had not intervened.

Joey became a Freeman of Ballymoney, and went on to assume an almost mythical status among road racing enthusiasts; such was the length and continued success of a career that started in 1969 on a lowly Triumph Tiger Cub. For the wider audience outside the Emerald Isle, he really sprang to prominence when winning the 1977 Jubilee Classic TT on the Rea 750 Yamaha. It was that performance that was to lead to him becoming the longest serving rider in any manufacturers' team when Honda commenced supplying him with machines in 1981 to contest the FI World Championship. Joey has ridden Hondas from 125 to 1123cc, from production machines to works exotica like the RVF's and won on them all. It has been a top-flight career only interrupted for any length of time by his very heavy Brands Hatch smash in 1989, when a crashing Stephane Mertens brought him down. If you were to have watched Joey at most of the more usual viewing places around the Isle of Man TT circuit, you might well decide that he was unspectacular and wonder how he achieved race winning speeds. Having been passed by him myself on just about every part of the course in my own long career, in the early days, I too wondered. The answer turned out to be a simple and, on reflection, an obvious one. There is little time to be saved by scratching that bit harder on a slow corner but through a high-speed section, the precision between the curbs and hedges revealed the man's genius.

Given Dunlop's sometimes retiring public persona, writing this competition biography represented something of a journalistic challenge. Joey was a reluctant hero, not given to the easy response of many another public figure. I therefore approached the task of writing this book by having to rely heavily upon those who have been part of his life - and escapades. Those who are part of the close knit Dunlop circle and lucky enough to have earned the right to refer to the man as a friend, have earned his trust over many years and are part of a family to which admittance is paid for in shared experience. Many of them have been kind enough to provide their own tributes in this work, which is my attempt to put the man on the page - a distillation, the essence of Dunlop. I thought long and hard before presuming to give my own opinion of Joey and what qualities made him what he was. But here it is along with those who knew him better than I did.

Joey was, perhaps surprisingly to the general public, a complex character. He would, on the one hand at a race meeting, seem reserved - introverted and withdrawn; certainly diffident when it came to talking to the media. On another occasion, he practically took charge of an Ulster television interview - when the fancy had taken him. He could be totally single-minded and focused upon a particular objective as to shut out the rest of the world. As a man, Joey was a uniquely self-motivated individual. There is almost no other racer I can think of who, on his day, could be so single minded and focused upon the race in hand. Money has never been his motivation. The man seemed quite bemused by all the publicity side of things, the corollary to that, was that he is totally unruffled by it all, too. The man is quite unique in modern day racing. It's a somewhat curious fact of life that many people like to see a top star beaten by an up and coming lad; knocked of his perch. They always cheer what is at the time the underdog, but with Joey over all the years it was different. They just seemed happy to see him out there. At the TT if he had a bad year, you heard fans say, 'well he's nothing to prove has he.' And when he did win, they were absolutely delighted, no matter who it was he had beaten.

As a character, he was sheer brilliance. What else can one say about someone who can find his own way to Romania or Bosnia all by himself and, in the middle of winter, without any problems that he himself couldn't solve on the spot. You would hardly guess that he was, in fact, a very shrewd, thinking man, with tremendous determination. A last thought that perhaps really reveals something of the man. At a recent TT while in the paddock, he said: 'I don't understand why all these people want my autograph, I just ride a motorbike well.'

If he chose to become involved in running supplies to Bosnia or wherever, he would happily live within himself for the weeks that it took him to drive single-handed, thousands of miles into uncertain territory, living out of his cab. He could, quite naturally, lead a small band of supporters across Europe. In the Langford Lough incident he was the man who emerged at the vital moment to take charge of rescuing the people on the boat. Shake the man by the hand and it was surprisingly soft and the grip gentle, but a moment's eye contact left me with the feeling that he'd got my number.

Having competed with, not against, Joey over the Mountain circuit for 17 years myself, I'd begun to gain an appreciation of, and admiration for, the Dunlop expertise. As a journalist in motorcycling since 1961, I had long wanted to tackle a book on Joey as my own personal tribute to the man.

As I was working on the last chapter, one of my Irish collaborators, Kenneth Boyd, rang to convey the tragic news of Joey's last race. I have refrained from changing tenses where quoting the anecdotes and experiences, all of which were given before this time.

'I just wanted to be myself. I never wanted to be a superstar.
I hope people will remember me that way.'

Acknowledgements

Special thanks for the valuable help given by Ivan Davidson, that lifelong fan, for allowing me to refer to his comprehensive compilation of Joey's racing results, without which I would have been unaware of many of his early performances.

In particular, I should thank John Harris, who in the early stages of putting this together, was both sponsoring myself and Joey on Honda CBR 600's. It was this that led me to meet many of the people I have drawn upon for stories about Joey, as well as those who I got to know through my own racing and journalistic career.

This book would be much the poorer without the reminiscences of:
Bob McMillan, Honda Racing Manager UK
Rex White, Suzuki Race Team Manager UK
Barry Symmons, who worked with Joey for many years through his F1 campaign
Hector Neill for his memories of Joey riding his 500 Suzuki
Andy Inglish - on being Joey's mechanic
Father, Willie Dunlop, Joey's early days with his Suzuki, when we met at Cookstown
Billy Nutt, organiser of the Pure Roads Series
Ron Haslam, on Joey as a team mate
Ray McCullough, another Irish road racing legend
Neil Tuxworth, Honda Race Team Manager
Terry Teece and Joey's Classic Manx Grand Prix rides
Nick Jefferies, Honda teammate
Robert Dunlop, living in the shadow of 'big brother'
Nigel McClatchey and Kenneth Boyd for their invaluable help in reading the typescript
and checking the 'Irish bits,' as well as adding items of which I was unaware.

Many of Joey's friends, supporters and acquaintances shun the limelight when talking about Joey, and prefer to remain anonymous. I thank them all for their contributions.

Ray Knight - a Joey fan, like all the others.
Isle of Man, November, 2000.

Mortons Motorcycle Media hope this book has brought you a little closer to the man who was without doubt, the king of road racing. This would not have been possible without the help of the following people who are listed in no particular order. We offer sincere apologies if anyone has been missed out:

Don Morley; Ian Kerr; Bill Snelling (FoTTofinders); TT Riders Association and Allan Robinson in particular; Karl Schleuter; Alan and Terry Wilson, Paul Smith - Redline Books; Malcolm Wheeler, Terry Clark - Mortons Motorcycle Media Ltd.

Publishing Director of Mortons Motorcycle Media Ltd and former TT racer, Malcolm Wheeler, explains how the book came about and the involvement of the TT Riders Association.

'It happened while standing in the paddock during TT 2000. Ray Knight and myself were indulging in that practice popular with old TT riders, that is analysing the current crop of brave young men tackling the worst that the Mountain Circuit could throw at them. We agreed this year was exceptional. Who could fail to be impressed by the likes of young David Jefferies? But the performance of one man, almost twice the age of many of his adversaries, left us both in awe. Joey Dunlop had just completed his third win of the week, and worked hard for them all.

'Not wanting to miss the moment, Ray told me of words he had spent almost ten years compiling, which make up the book you are now holding in your hand, and offered me the chance to publish it through the company for which I work, Mortons Motorcycle Media Ltd. I readily accepted.

'Neither of us could have predicted the terrible events that were to follow, almost before the TT dust had settled.

'With the encouragement of the TT Riders Association, the enthusiasm of my colleague Terry Clark, designers and printers Alan and Terry Wilson of Redline Books, and of course Ray himself, we took the decision to press on. We are all proud to have played a part in the finished work.'

Malcolm Wheeler.
Publishing Director, Mortons Motorcycle Media Ltd.

A donation has been made to the TT Riders Association to be used in Joey's memory, by the following people involved in the production of this book.
Ray Knight - Author
Mortons Motorcycle Media Limited - Publishers
Redline Books - Design and Print
Don Morley - Photographer.

HONDA

From Cub racer to record breaker

1968-75

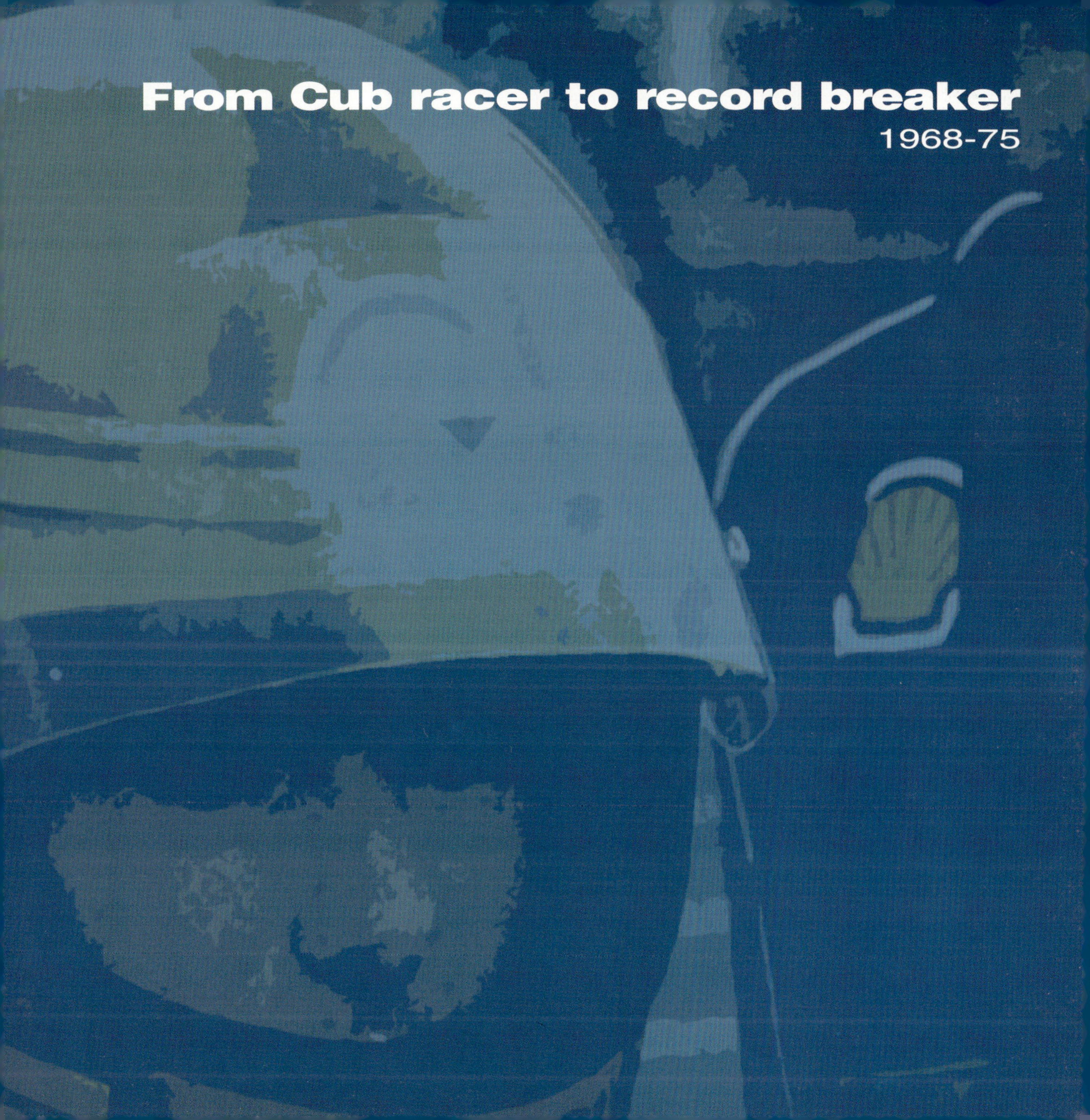

Before making a racing debut, Joey had taken to the Irish roads on a C15 Beeza. In fact, Joey never passed his motorcycle test until the late 1980s. A motorcycle was what every Irish lad of the time just had to have; it was the pathway to speed, excitement and adventure. Negotiating the tortuous lanes surrounding Ballymoney at ever-faster speeds led to a familiarity with the adrenaline rush generated by controlling a bike at speed. Joey hardly needed the example and encouragement of friend Mervyn Robinson, who was already racing, to take his own place on the grid.

The short circuit at Lurgan Park in August 1969 was where a 17-year-old Joe Dunlop first turned wheels on racing tarmac. Those who watched the heats of the 200cc race would have seen the 199cc Triumph carry Joe to victory and with a win under his belt first time out, he then went on to finish 4th in the final. The men who preceded him in his first race were Anthony Owens and Bobby Whyte riding Bultacos and Eddie Farmer on another Cub; a promising start indeed.

Washing down engines and being general dogsbody in the haulage company where his Father Willie worked, enabled Joey to earn just enough money to put the Cub onto the grid for the second time that year. It was in September at the Carrowdore 100 road meeting where Alan Crozier, on a 196 Suzuki, took top spot. Bobby Whyte was second again and the third place went to J.Fletcher. Both rode 'Bultos' but this time it was Stanley McKee who got his Cub home ahead of Joey's.

Joey had had to borrow £50 to buy that little Triumph. But just making the repayments on the loan meant that he had to restrict his race programme to two races in his first season. While that simple machine was the starting point of an illustrious career, it was somewhat fated. And it was to wreck not only his 1970 season but was itself wrecked and not by Joey. It was the Easter Monday meeting at Kirkistown when another motorist driving a Mini, crashed into him writing off his Mini, trailer and Cub.

Joey was to join the rising tide of Japanese two-stroke technology for the 1971 season, choosing to replace the Cub with a Suzuki with which to contest the 200cc races; a popular class in Ireland designed with the impecunious clubman in mind. Out at Kirkistown for the Easter meeting, his first ride on the Suzuki earned him another fourth place as Owens once more took the win. However, the following meeting at Bishopscourt in April was memorable for a couple of reasons. Joey only finished in seventh place at that meeting but the winner of the class was non-other than a very young Barry Sheene on the ex-works 125 Suzuki that was to bring him so much success. Once more Owens and Whyte beat him to the flag but just in front of Joey was a man who would later feature largely in the career of the budding world champion road racer - David Wood. And of all things, he was riding a Triumph Cub!

The Tandragee 100 was next and the Suzy brought success with a second place in the 200 race and a win in the Handicap event. But behind the results lies a story in itself. When Joey had started the bike in the paddock for practice it had bent a connecting rod. Willie Dunlop, Joe's dad, takes up the story. 'The fuel taps had been left on overnight and fuel had run down through the carburettor into the crankcase. The bike wouldn't start at first but instead of draining the sump, they insisted on pushing it until it fired. The consequences were disastrous. With the crankcase full of fuel, when the motor fired up, the connecting rod had nowhere to go and just had to bend; they were lucky the fuel did not ignite and blow the motor apart. So Mervyn (Robinson) and I stripped the engine, found a couple of large ring spanners and levering one against the other, bent the connecting rod somewhere near straight to get him onto the grid.'

The Cookstown 100 followed in May and Joey's Suzuki chased home the Bultacos of Whyte and Tom Finlay and it was Whyte again at the Maghaberry Circuit the following month who once more got to 'the line' first with Owens in attendance, Joey third. However, the budding racer's cash now ran out and those five meetings were all that the man could afford to contest. He would have to wait with mounting impatience right round to the April of 1972 before he could once more twist the grip in anger.

Now while the 1972 season would not actually bring Joey any particular success, his employer, Danny McCook, who ran a small local haulage business, was taking a growing interest in Joey's budding road racing career. Joey would work as a mechanic on the vehicles and sometimes drive them,

delivering coal around Ballymoney. Danny would come to the meetings and his support would soon blossom into sponsorship. But before that fortunate occurrence, the overbored 125 to 182cc Hondas were becoming popular in the class and they would prove to be more than a match for the Suzukis. It was at the season's opener at Maghaberry, that Jackie Robinson took the 200 class honours with another of the little four-stroke twins in second place ridden by Sam Dempster. By now, the 200cc class was becoming increasingly competitive and Joey struggled to come home sixth.

At the same venue in June it was back to 'normal results' with Bobby Whyte again doing the business on his Bultaco with Dunlop third behind Richard Hewitt on another Suzy. At Lurgan Park it was Dempster's turn to win with Micky Laverty chasing him on a similar machine; Joey another sixth. Joey finished the season by taking in the Mid-Antrim 150 for the first time and while fifth was not too much to shout about, it was worth noting the appearance of Raymond Hanna behind him on a Bulto and he would certainly go on to make a name for himself.

It has to be said that at this stage after four years at the game, Dunlop was yet to show the form or results that would bring sponsors queuing up at his garage door but Danny thought he recognised obvious winning potential in the man. During that winter, Danny and Joey put their heads together and took a hard look at the machines that were available at an acceptable price and the races to be contested. In the early seventies, the 350 class was regarded as pretty competitive and it was this that they chose as the route to international competition. Unfortunately, while the chosen Aermacchi's simple four-stroke engine had recently powered many another racer to the front of the pack, in performance terms it was about to be overtaken by the seed of the burgeoning Japanese motorcycle industry, the 350 Yamaha two-stroke twin.

Danny's backing removed the financial constraints that had held Joey back from contesting more races in the past and having the cash available with which to persuade more brake horses from the Suzuki. The Aermacchi was not ready in time for the first meeting of 1973 at Maghaberry and Joey finished sixth on the Suzy. Fifth was that man Davy Wood on a 182 Honda, like the second man home, Sam Dempster, and the winner similarly equipped was another name in the making - Courtney Junk.

When Joey lined up the Macchi for his first race in the 350 event at Tandragee, he was faced by some formidable opposition. To finish sixth behind winner Gerry Mateer, Tom Herron and Gordon Bell, all on Yamahas, with Joe McArdle fourth on a Macchi and Drew Alexander fifth on another Yamaha, could be counted as a most successful debut ride in that class of competition.

Mervyn Robinson had in many ways been Joey's mentor, his own racing activities acting like a magnet in attracting Joey to take the plunge. It was at Mondello Park in May, in the Monarch of Mondello Race, that Joey Dunlop beat his teacher on an identical bike to take fourth place as, Englishman Martin Sharpe took the win on his Yamaha. Bob Sherman was second on a 250 model and Donal Cormican completed the rostrum on the first four-stroke. The Handicap race saw Joey in third spot as Sharpe did it again with Cormican second.

A young Joey Dunlop dressed in black as part of the Honda team protest in 1981.

Perhaps Joey's debut in the North West 200 is one he would rather forget. On the start line, the chain of the Aermacchi broke, leaving him to watch the field disappearing into the distance. However, racing on the limit inevitably means exceeding it sooner or later and Joey tasted the tarmac at Maghaberry while dicing with local ace Campbell Gorman. He bit the dust and broke his first bone, that 'favourite' of road racers, his collarbone. Joey was not going to be deterred by such a trivial injury though and with the enthusiasm of youth, was back on the grid just three weeks later at the Mid-Antrim 150. In spite of the barely healed injury, Joey raced to seventh.

In a first appearance at the Ulster Grand Prix, while Joey managed to beat all the other four-strokes in the race, he could finish no higher than an inauspicious 19th but in a truly talented international field headed by winner John Williams, chased home by Tony Rutter and Charlie Williams. Kirkistown, Maghaberry, Fore and Mid-Antrim followed quickly with Joey being busier than he'd ever had the opportunity to be before. He beat Mervyn at Kirkistown to finish fifth but Mervyn turned the tables at Maghaberry as Campbell Gorman and Tom Herron duelled in first and second. Fourth at Fore followed as the leading four-stroke, to be repeated at Mid-Antrim similarly but down in seventh place. First four-stroke was really the best result that could be expected from here on in as Yamahas now packed the grids.

It was, perhaps, a portent of things to come when a first visit across the Irish Sea to start his Isle of Man racing career, provided him with a second and two third places on the Jurby Road circuit; one on which I was somewhat heavily, to conclude my own career 22 years later. This was quite something of an adventure as the trip was made in a local fishing boat and would have an echo - though something of a unfortunate one, in a trip to the TT in later years.

A couple more meetings at Maghaberry's short circuit rounded off the season with places as high as a second spot but this was only possible where power deficiencies could be offset by out scratching the opposition. That fact was not to go unnoticed by Danny McCook and for the 1974 season he expressed his faith in his protégé in the most concrete terms by equipping Joey with the necessary machinery for success, an air-cooled 350 Yamaha for the coming season. This was to be the year when Joey came of age in racing terms, displaying an emerging talent that enabled him to contest a season-long battle with Mervyn, Cambell Gorman, Abe Alexander and Ian McGregor.

It didn't take Joey Dunlop long to get the hang of riding a two-stroke to its limit and after third and fourth at Kirkistown he scored a win, second and third places at Maghaberry. That good start to the season was perhaps a little premature as it took Joey right through to September at Maghaberry again before winning from Sam McClements and finishing second to Mervyn in the Embassy Championship Race. That man Wood appeared in the results again but in fourth spot on a 250. Those two wins were all that he could count in season '74 but places came thick and fast among all the names of the day. There was a second to Alexander in the Leinster 200, beating Mervyn and Ray McCullough. Third in the Cookstown 100 to Tom Herron and Mervyn followed, a second to Ian McGregor at Kirkistown and second to Mervyn at Fore. The season was concluded by Mervyn Robinson and Joey taking the ferry to Scotland for the end of season meeting at Knockhill. The trip

A young Joe Dunlop, he still carried that name on the fairing, caught in pensive mood on the start line at the TT.

proved to be most worthwhile as they made the 350 race their own, finishing at the front and in that order.

Those early Yamahas were not noted for their road holding over the jumps and bumps of Irish road circuits, whereas Colin Seeley framed AJS and Matchless machines had long since set the standards in places like the Isle of Man as well as on the UK short circuits. Joey now fitted his Yamaha motor into a Seeley frame, the first of several.

A happy and relaxed Joey Dunlop, no doubt trying hard to become a public relations man while sporting the Honda Britain leathers.

Joey's riding abilities were maturing for all to see during 1974 and while Danny was helping Joey as much as he was able, his results and obvious potential attracted the attention of the Rea brothers and with their greater resources they would open more opportunities for Joey in 1975. Joey opened his 1975 racing campaign by taking in a UK visit to the Croft short circuit and when you consider that the 350 race was won by Kork Ballington, chased home by Roger Marshall, Joey in third place, returned to the Emerald Isle extremely satisfied with the result. On to Kirkistown and if sixth doesn't sound like an auspicious start to the Irish season that year, the fast and furious dicing that produced a win for Ray McCullough, followed by Mervyn, Alexander, Campbell Gorman and Sam McClements, has to be appreciated. Joey still had the little Suzuki and ran it at Aghadowey for another sixth but the 350 came good taking him to a splendid second, albeit behind Mervyn again but in front of McCullough, Gordon Bell and Campbell Gorman. And for good measure, a third in the Embassy Championship race rounded off the day.

Mondello Park in May saw a little piece of history as Joey recorded his first double victory in winning the 350 race in front of Mervyn and the Unlimited event, on what was listed as a 351 Yamaha, in front of the 354 Sparton of Bob Stevenson and Danny's similarly enlarged Yamaha. That double was a reflection of the growing support of the Rea brothers John, Neil and Martin. And it was a double win again at the St.Angelo short circuit before going to the Tandragee where a fine battle with Ray McCullough ensued as Joey finished second.

Joey's performance at the Tandragee had left the Rea brothers totally enthused with their foray into sponsorship and they acquired a water-cooled unit for the 500. Now Joey had two machines and could contest all the major races on competitive machinery, but if greater success seemed imminent, in racing there's always many a slip!

With high hopes, the Reas' and Joey's now growing band of supporters arrived at the 1975 North West 200 but the vital element in any racer's armory is luck - Lady Luck was not in the team for this meeting. The 500 blew up in practice and the 350 seized on the first lap of the race at Portrush. With the Cookstown 100 meeting following on the heels of the

North West, parts with which to repair the 500 could not be obtained in time so a DNS (Did Not Start) was recorded, and just for good measure the 350 again seized.

The 350 was just not living up to its potential and the Rea brothers, with the view that it might well continue to spoil their rider's career prospects, took the bull by the horns and obtained a new 350 engine and Seeley frame. Joey assembled the bike and gave it its debut at the 'King of Kirkistown' meeting with resounding success. In winning what was to become the first of many 'man of the meeting' titles, Joey rewarded his sponsors with a string of wins at Mondello Park.

The King of Kirkistown title followed as he was now regularly beating the hard men of Irish racing but then that man Ray McCullough relegated him to two seconds in the Skerries meeting and their regular personal battle raged high. As something of a footnote, another TT winner in the making, Nick Jefferies appears in the results with fourth and fifth behind them.

There is a personal memory of that Skerries meeting, related by Frank Lyons in the pages of the April issue of *Motorcycle Sport*. 'I took up my usual position along a stretch of the road known as Shady Lane, a fast, bumpy and downhill section just past the start/finish line. Prior to that meeting I had seen a couple of dozen meetings but nothing quite prepared me for what I saw that day. The sight of Dunlop and Robinson cresting the hill side-by side and virtually, if not actually banging fairings, was absolutely breathtaking. Ray McCullough went by quicker, but these two thirds of the Armoy Armada were so wild and ragged that they looked incredibly fast and were exciting in the extreme.'

Something that was to become a habit started at the Temple 100 where Joey cracked in a new lap record on his way to winning the 500 race on the '351.' Then it was doubles time again at Aghadowey with 350 and 500 wins and then on to the Mid-Antrim for another win and lap record. He was in unstoppable form now and recorded a 'triple top' in cleaning up the Unlimited, Invitation and 350 races and each time it was Mervyn Robinson who chased him home. But he didn't take that lying down and beat Joey at the following meeting at Mondello in the Experts Race.

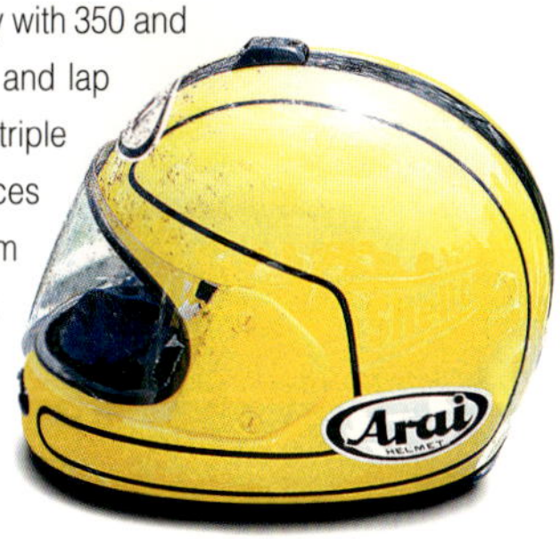

The RC30 shows the scars of yet another duel and a million flies are testimony to Joey's high speed laps.

Joey's riding skills were now becoming nicely honed. However, at the Ulster Grand Prix, left at the start and with a full head of adrenaline to spur his pursuit of the leaders, he rode over the fine edge on lap three. He had fought his way right through the field to third place, only to crash out and break that collar bone again.

Healed once more, Joey went back to the now familiar Mondello venue to win the Monarch of Mondello title. On to the Carrowdore 100 and Aghadowey meetings for a pair of 350 and 500 doubles came next. September continued to be a busy month with a further win at Mondello and then a visit across the water to Croft once more where this time the English were equal to the challenge as Mervyn slotted into third place behind Haynes and Batty with Joey in fourth.

It was something of a grand finale to the season at the familiar Kirkistown meet in October. Ray won the Embassy Championship Race as Joey and Mervyn followed him, albeit somewhat furiously. Mervyn's 350 win saw Ray follow Joey and the 500 event was a Dunlop victory in front of Sammy McClements and Gerry Mateer. The scene is described in the Armoy Armada's Supporters magazine, recording in the Embassy Final race, that Joey, in an inspired last lap, last corner move, sneaked in front of Ray McCullough. But he was pushing just that little bit too hard and ran wide; Ray snatched back the lead and the win with Joey practically riding pillion.

1975 concluded with there being no doubt that Joey had, in racing terms, come of age. With the Rea brothers' support providing him with top class machinery, he proved that he could take on and beat the best. 1976 would start his Isle of Man apprenticeship and with it build the foundations of a career that would bring multiple World Championships.

The Armoy Armada

Mervyn, Frank, Jim and Joey

That the Irish are enthusiastic supporters of road racing there can be little doubt. Anyone who has witnessed the crowds that come to the North West 200 and Ulster Grand Prix meetings must agree; anywhere from 80 - 100,000 spectators have been quoted as the likely number attending. Certainly at the '200', as a competitor with tunnel vision myself, I would be aware of, and spurred on by, their presence.

There are plenty of examples of supporters groups being formed to assist their chosen causes. One could do little better than to quote the example of the Ulster Grand Prix Supporters' Club, without which the financial support it gives each year, the future of the race must seriously be in doubt. More specifically and as it comes into this story, there is the Armoy Armada Supporters Club. This was formed in 1977 and came out of a conversation among a group of motorcycle road racing fanatics about three local riders, all men from Armoy - Joey, Mervyn Robinson and Frank Kennedy. The aforesaid group agreed that these three men had played a great part in what was fast becoming a resurgence in Irish racing and were deserving of their support. This 'team' collectively acquired the name of the Armoy Armada, and their battles with the Dromara Destroyers comprised of Ray McCullough, Brian Reid and Trevor Steele, became legendary. So was the cut and thrust between the riders and badinage over quantities of the 'Liffy water' between the opposing supporters.

The conversation had taken place in the Railway Tavern, which had established itself as something of an impromptu clubhouse for many an unofficial meeting of like-minded enthusiasts. Fate must have been playing a part in those circumstances because in the course of time, Joey would become Landlord of the Railway, later to become Joey's Bar. Conversation flowed as it usually does on such occasions and out of it came the formation of the Club with the aim of helping the three riders; Jim Dunlop was also beginning to display an emerging talent, indeed he subsequently became one of the supported members.

The first means of raising cash for their riders, was to have a membership fee of £2.00 plus dues of a £1 per month. Just to show how active the club became, they even managed to persuade the likes of ex-world champion Ralph Bryans to put in an appearance at a club night. Other famous names who were persuaded to support the Club's drive for such a worthy cause were Dick Creith of Bushmills, who was famous for his performances on the Ryan 'Fireplace' Nortons, and Len Ireland, one of his greatest rivals. These two men were Irish racing legends in their own era.

Such was the success of the club from its inception that it was able to guarantee each of its four riders £100 towards the season of 1977. This first season of very successful racing support started to convince the general public that they really were set to do great things for Irish road racing because for 1978 they were able to raise their guarantee to the riders to £200 as membership rapidly rose. The Club's success was not just confined to supporting their chosen four riders though. With the thought that they could do even more to promote Irish road racing, they then sponsored a race at Aghadowey, as it was the nearest circuit to their 'headquarters'. They chose a title for the race, 'Ace of Aghadowey' and the prize fund to be paid was no less than £215, the cash was paid right down to tenth place, plus suitable silverware. Joey promptly won the title, Frank finished seventh and brother Jim was tenth; the Club was naturally over the moon and the results spurred them to even greater efforts.

Enthused with this success, the Club then set about raising funds for the following year's race and to this end they were able to put up a GS750 Suzuki for the top prize in a draw, with a second of a TS100 Trail Suzuki. The resounding result was no less than £1,500 for the coming season. This did not change the Club's policy of supporting their riders though, and each of the four was to receive £500 per man. One more instance of the initiatives the Club came up with was to have badges and tee shirts made and these items proved to be very popular fund-raisers. Hard working club committee members, Tommy Louden and Billy Gillan, were largely responsible for this exercise.

As well as the many fund-raising activities organised to bring in the cash for the team's race budget, the sponsor list for that year was as follows: Rea Transport, Hugh O'Kane (Motors), Samuel Taggart - Plant and Machinery Sales,

Martin Rea - Sawmills, Mervyn Turtle Ltd - Car Sales, Sylvia Turtle Fashions and J.McMaster & Sons - Elf Oil distributors. Mention must also be made of Lawrence Kelly, owner of the Railway Tavern, who gave the Club a room every Wednesday night and who put up the 'Man of the Year' award in 1977; and it was won by Joey! Norman Cantley, of the Langholm Hotel, boosted the prize fund for the Ace of Aghadowey and no less enthusiastic supporters were Maurice McCaughan, Wallace Patton, Samuel Anderson and Alistair Patrick. And as the Armoy Supporter's Club magazine for 1978 put it: 'There are many more who have given money and helped in various ways and to them the Club are indebted and could not have executed many of their ventures without their contributions.'

This chapter would not be complete without profiles on the rest of the Armoy Armada; Mervyn, Frank and Jim. I unearthed a copy of the original *Armoy Armada Newsletter* that revealed much of the activities and enthusiasm of the time. Priced at 60p, it is undated and published some time in 1978. Edited by Mel Murphy, Chairman and Editor, it did not have a follow-up. It provided much information on Joey's early racing years and has also been drawn upon heavily for these profiles.

Mervyn (Robo) Robinson

Mervyn was one of a group of exceptionally talented road racers that led to something approaching a rebirth of Irish racing in the late 60s and through the 70s on into 1980. Names like Ray McCullough, Tom Herron, Norman Brown, Donny Robinson, Brian Reid, Sam McClements, Steven Cull, Con Law, Campbell Gorman and Connor McGinn, are obvious other candidates; the list could be much longer.

★ JOHN REA. Who is Joey's sponsor owns the haulage firm of Rea Transport, in Templepatrick & has lived in America for some time. Surely the greatest moment for John was when Joey won the Jubilee Race in the Isle of Man & it goes without saying how everyone felt for John in his moment of triumph and how proud he must have felt of his Rea Racing Team which could not have deserved any less than this great victory.

★ SAM TAGGART. Who runs a Plant & Equipment Sales brought the first 500cc Sparton into N. I. & Frank Kennedy had hard luck not winning the N.W. 200 with Sams machine. At the end of the '77 season Joey Dunlop took 2nd at Kirkistown after starting at the back of the grid & led the 500 race at Aghadowey until the last lap at the chicane when the joining link in the chain broke, so victory eluded the Sparton once again but 1978 could prove different. Sam Taggart has done it again and purchased a 1978 250cc Yamaha for Joey Dunlop & its first race was at Daytona & finished 8th.

There are only a few of the sponsors of this magnificent sport which could not continue without their devotion & ability to spend £1000's of pounds with no return year after year.

★ HUGH O'KANE. Who is Mervyn Robinsons' sponsor and has year after year provided a machine for his rider, but surely his greatest moment was when Mervyn won the 1975 500cc race at the U.G.P. & I am sure that Hugh will look back in years to come on it as a great day in his life. When not watching his rider Hugh runs a car sales business in Armoy & is now the agent for Skoda G.B. in the North Antrim area.

★ VICTOR FREEMAN. Team Manager of Rea Racing has now devoted part of his time to arranging Joey's meetings and guiding his career. Victor is probably more famous for his work in helping run the N.W.200

★ MERVYN TURTLE. Who is also sponsor for Frank Kennedy runs a car sales business out side Ballymena & purchased a new 350 Cantilever Yamaha for Frank last year but bad luck struck & as you have read in Franks' profile he had to retire for the rest of the season because of injury, but '78 is a new season.

★ MARTIN REA. Brother of John Rea & is now Jim Dunlop's sponsor. He bought Joey's old Yamsel for Jim last year & mid way through the season bought a new 350 engine & for 1978 has got Jim another bike to contest in two classes. Martin owns a Sawmill Works in Moira.

Mervyn's career started a year before Joey's initial foray into the sport in 1969, but his career commenced on something unusual, a machine powered by a twin cylinder two-stroke from Villiers. It was called an FKS Special, quite simply because Frank Kennedy had built it and he persuaded Frank to let him borrow his creation. The Cookstown meeting was the scene of Mervyn's debut, followed by the Killinchy and Mid-Antrim meetings, the hotbed of Irish racing at the time.

Fired up with enthusiasm after his first three rides, he set about construction of his own bike and the result was the ever-popular Triumph

Mervyn Robinson was without doubt a major influence on Joey's earlier career.

Tiger Cub. However, he did not manage to put it onto the grid until the start of the 1970 season so in this he was following in Joey's footsteps.

The big break came in 1972 when friend Hugh O'Kane asked Mervyn if he wanted to try his hand at building up an old 7R AJS he had lying in bits in his garage. His talent as a mechanic was obvious in the assembled racer and Hugh was so impressed that he let Mervyn race the bike at Kirkistown on Easter Monday as payment for the job that he had done. Success followed at Mid-Antrim where he gained his first trophy on the bike with a fifth in the 500 class; this was quickly the start of a successful association between rider and sponsor.

On something of a high, an entry was quickly secured for the Isle of Man September races and off went Hugh and Mervyn to the Manx Grand Prix; and Hugh liked very much what he saw. That valuable booklet, 'History of the Manx Grand Prix,' succinctly records that Mervyn retired the Ajay in the Junior. Not to be deterred though, Hugh purchased a 350 Aermacchi in the Island and brought it back with him determined to be ready for the 1973 season.

Mervyn started brilliantly on the 'Macchi at the NW 200 by being the first four-stroke home in his class - like Joe, he got his hands on a quick four-stroke at a time when they were becoming less competitive against the rising tide of strokers. However, fate intervened at this stage because after Mervyn put up a cracking show at the Temple 100, a buyer approached Hugh to purchase the bike and would not take no for an answer. If that temporarily put a cloud on Mervyn's racing horizon, then it really had a silver lining as with the cash - and some, Hugh bought Billy McCosh's air cooled Yamaha for him to ride.

Joey never felt totally at home in front of the camera unless he was astride a motorcycle. In this shot he gives the photographer a rather wistful smile.

The best results scored by Mervyn in the later part of '73 were third at Carrowdore after a very bad start and he was lying fourth in the Embassy Final when a back marker brought him off on the last lap of the race. However, Hugh O'Kane was so determined that his protégé should have the most competitive machinery affordable that he again acquired one of Billy's bikes; this time a water-cooled version of the Yamaha, for 1974. It obviously proved to be an inspired move because Mervyn promptly won his first race on the bike, and to quote the Newsletter once more: 'In fact he won three altogether at the Isle of Man Jurby Road Races. Celebrations lasted until the next morning with brother-in-law Joey Dunlop playing his part as barman!'

Mervyn's first Irish road race was at Kirkistown when he won the Embassy Race. At Fore he won 'most of the races' and with fastest laps for good measure, brought home a bag full of silverware. Hugh O'Kane sought to enjoy even more success and subsequently bought back Mervyn's old air-cooled Yamaha and converted it to an oversize so as to be able to compete in the 500 class as well. The rest of the season was good but best of all was to finish the year at Carrowdore where he took the 350 race from Billy Guthrie and a win in the Embassy final on the 350.

Into season 1975 and a fastest lap in practice for the NW 200 was mute testimony to Mervyn's capabilities but a seizure meant a hasty rebuild before the race in which an excellent sixth against top competition could only be very good. If that was a good performance, then the following

Ulster GP was a real career highlight. In what was described as cruel weather, Mervyn beat Tony Rutter, himself at the peak of his career, by a handsome distance and Tony commented after the race: 'Mervyn was the best man on the day.' It was a performance that persuaded William Shaw of Rent-a-Skip, Ballymena, to offer sponsorship for 1976. But to round off that season, there was a memorable meeting in the Embassy Final where Mervyn, Ray McCullough and Joey diced all the way through and the race was decided on the last corner with Ray getting the verdict by going through on the inside of the pair. For good measure in the 350 race, Mervyn won, to relegate Joey to second.

The Ulster Grand Prix saw Mervyn make a particularly bad start and after being in 24th place on the first lap, finally battled through to sixth and bettered that with 3rd in the 500 race behind Stan Woods on the works Suzuki, and Joey himself. The 1977 season was not a good one for Mervyn. Riding Sam Taggart's Sparton at St.Angelo, Mervyn took a bad toss, hitting a pole and sustaining concussion that sidelined him for most of the season. As if that were not bad enough, making a return at the end of that year, another incident resulted in a badly damaged knee. Gritty determination best describes his comeback in which he won the 500 race at Carrowdore and the title of '50 Mile Champion.'

Mervyn was killed in the 1980 North West, an event that so affected Joey and his family that he seriously considered retirement. Joey subsequently went to Cookstown and won what he called 'a tribute to his brother-in-law.'

Frank Kennedy

Frank started his motorcycling career in 1971 and he too borrowed the 7R Ajay from Hugh O'Kane and scored several thirds and fourths. However, he was determined to get his own bike. Frank in fact did buy Gordon Bell's Aermacchi, finished ten races and was 'always first four-stroke home.' After that promising start he took a bad tumble when out testing, hitting a large stone at 120mph. His numerous internal injuries and a broken leg, put him on the critical list for several days. He was actually kept in hospital for five months and had to use crutches until 1973.

However, with the grittiness exemplified by Irish roadracers, this was only a temporary setback and he made it back to racing at the Tandragee 100 that same year and finished seventh on a Manx Norton. After this, Frank progressed to two-stroke machinery and scored several places, including runner-up spot to Campbell Gorman at Maghaberry and he seemed to have arrived with that performance. 1974 saw him end the season as 500 Short Circuit Champion.

For 1975, Sam Taggart and Mervyn Turtle took Frank under their wing and Frank had new 350 and 500 machines to put on the grid and success came quickly with Frank winning the 500cc class Road Racing & Short Circuit Championships. That achievement was not without incident though as at the Temple 100 Frank took another bad toss and he had to fight his way back to fitness once more to claim sixth place at the Ulster.

Frank's talent really came to the fore in 1976, when on Sam's new Sparton three-cylinder racer and the first of its kind in Ireland, he stormed off into a seventeen second lead in the North West before ignition gremlins struck to let top English racer Martin Sharpe take the win. He confessed afterwards that there was no way that he could have caught Frank; Suzuki rider Percy Tait was similarly embarrassed.

Frank certainly suffered enough injuries in his short career. Following a blitz of the Isle of Man Jurby races, both on the road and Airfield circuits, he then went to the Mid-Antrim 150. It was while dicing with fellow Armoy Armada team member Mervyn, that a mechanical fault caused him to tumble and break a collar bone which was slow to heal, forcing him to miss that year's Ulster.

Lady Luck was little kinder in 1977, as while riding Mervyn Turtle's new cantilever 350 Yamaha, a stone jammed in the carbs and caused the accident in which he broke both arms and was out for the rest of the year. Frank died competing in the 1979 North West 200.

Jim Dunlop

'Jim could have been better than any of us if he hadn't had the big crash', says Joey looking back on Jim's short career. Jim actually started racing later than the rest of the Armada, in fact in 1975 and on Joey's 200

Suzuki; he managed to get the loan of the bike because big brother wouldn't sell it to him. Success was immediate with his first appearance at Mondello Park with a second place to Sammy Dempster in the 200cc Final race, having relegated Adrian Craig to third and being spotted by Martin Rea trying to pass him on the grass!

Jim raced the Suzuki for quite a while with class wins at Knockhill and Cookstown. Most of the time that Jim raced the little Suzuki, he had to borrow the barrels off Dad's bike and replace them later in the day so that Willie could go to work on his bike.

"Racer" of 1976 and also the 30 lap race at Phoenix Park which had not been run since 1958 on a machine borrowed from Adrain Craig who finished second.

The 1976 season had now finished but all Joey was interested in was the new season to come. John Rea was Joey's sponsor as Noel & Martin found their own riders and this combination called REA RACING was ready to make the motor cycle world sit up and take notice.

John purchased the ex-Pat Mahoney 750cc Yamaha which was a 700cc orginally but had been converted to the larger capacity and after trying the bike at Oulton Park Joey decided to change the engine into a Seeley frame which had been built for a 500 Suzuki - quite a job, but the combination proved very successful also in the line-up of new machines was a 350 Cantilever Yamaha 1976 model & a 250 Yamsel which Joey prepared himself.

Joey had 33 wins, 16 seconds and five thirds in his Irish season which ended with him winning 3 short circuit championships 250, 350 & 750. Some of the titles he won were: "Embassy Champion" "King of Kirkistown", "Ace of Aghadowey", "Sunflower Champion", "Skerries", "Shell Sport Champion", and in the Isle of Man, "Southern 100 Champion" and his greatest success to date the "Schwepps Jubilee T.T. Race".

Throughout last season Joey seemed to do nothing but smash records and his greatest feat of the year must have been his 110.97 m.p.h. around the 37 and three quarter mile T.T. Course in the Isle of Man to be the third fastest ever.

At home he was the first rider ever to win four Short Circuit races on the same day & he went on to the King of Kirkistown meeting to make it 5 out of 5 in the one day!

To tell all the success of this rider one would need to write a book on him alone, but history will write itself given time and now Joey's only ambition is to do well in the 1978 season.

For this season John Rea has purchased a 1978 Model OW31 (750) Yamaha & a 350 Yam. Sam Taggart has supplied a new 250cc Yamaha. His first race was the Daytona 200 in the U.S.A. His racing calendar will include the most of the Road races at home and the Best 33 Championship, the Isle of Man and some Continental races.

Although Joey overshadows his fellow Armoy Armada team mates let's not under estimate the rest of the lads.

Frustration best describes his 1976 season as he acquired a TR2B 350 Yamaha, which broke down at every meeting. Halfway through '76, Jim gave up on it and built up a TR3 version which as it turned out was only just a little more reliable. But Joey took pity on him and lent him his water-cooled model, which he rode into fifth spot in a 500 race.

Jim went to work in England in 1977 so as to be able to earn enough cash to buy Joey's old TR3. But on returning home, he was over the moon to find out that that Martin Rea had already bought the bike and asked Jim to ride it for him. Now his racing career really took off and by the end of that season he had won the award for the 'Best Up and Coming Rider' of the year after places and wins from competing at Oulton and Cadwell Park, Tandragee, Cookstown and Mid-Antrim. It was here that he 'binned it' while dicing with Mervyn for fourth place but was lucky only to receive bruising. The Manx Grand Prix might well have really been the icing on the cake that year as he was placed sixth overall and the leading newcomer with a lap and a bit to go when the nut came off the clutch housing and Jim failed to finish.

Fate was cruel to Jim though, because the big crash and retirement was to follow to cut short a promising career.

Island apprentice

the first win

1976-1977

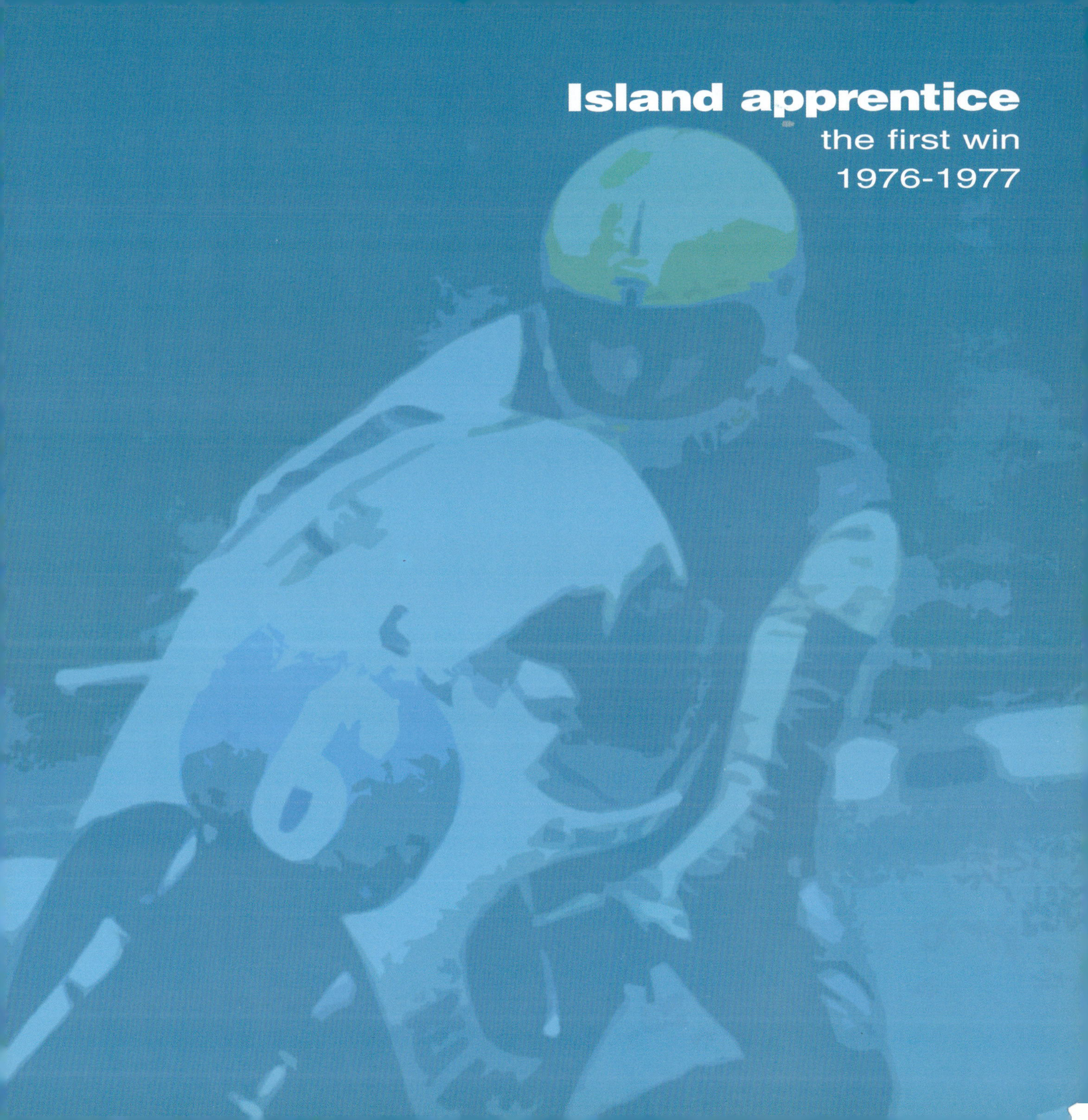

This was the year when Joey Dunlop really began to widen his racing horizons. His first race in 1976 was not in Ireland but in the UK, at Oulton Park. As the only issue of the Armoy Supporters Club magazine records the story, it was an illuminating experience that resulted from Joey being left for dead at the start of the race. With an empty road in front of him by the time the bike did fire up, Joey resigned himself to using the race laps to gain greater familiarity with a circuit that was still new to him. He was therefore not in full race mode when he overtook another back marker who was himself 'cruising.'

The overtaken rider promptly passed Joey back, to his considerable surprise. But no racer actually relishes being passed even if it is at the back of the field at the time and he responded by engaging a 'faster gear' to return the compliment. The mystery rider now proceeded to get his head down and in slipping back in front again, displayed a greater familiarity with the subtleties of Oulton Park. The rest of the race was spent by them both working up to a pace that must surely have seen them up with the front runners, that is if they had set off with them. Joey was by now so into the spirit of the occasion that he just had to find out who he'd had such a good race with. Searching the paddock for the number of the machine he'd sparred with, he was gratified to find that it belonged to non other than Charlie Williams, a man who had by then firmly established himself as a top UK runner. The race results show that the winner of that 500 race was Wayne Dinham, also on a 351 Yamaha, preceding Percy Tait on a 500 Suzuki, Eddie Roberts and John Cowie also rode oversized Yams.

The Dunlop bandwagon really began to roll this year on the Irish roads and circuits, but the year was most notable for his first appearance on the Isle of Man TT Mountain course. Willie Dunlop had accompanied Mervyn Robinson to the previous year's Manx Grand Prix and had become an instant convert to the atmosphere surrounding the event. He returned full of enthusiasm for Mona's Isle and with Joey's sponsor, John Rea being father of TT winner Johnny, it was almost a forgone conclusion that Joey would make his TT debut the following year. In the run up to that significant event, the Irish campaign was something of a triumph as Joey battled with Ray, Mervyn, Frank Kennedy and

Steve Cull. But Ray could still put it across Joey even when 'Yer Maun' was scoring two wins in a day, Ray seemed to snatch the Embassy Final Races and Steve Cull would sometimes take second spot for good measure. Joey was now contesting three classes as Sam Taggart added a 250 Yamaha to his stable. The results of the May Cookstown meeting records him finishing third on it behind Ian McGregor and that man McCullough again.

Early 'footage' of Joey on the 350cc Yamsel at Jurby airfield, Isle of Man in 1976.

Taking the fishing boat route, Joey was a late arrival in the Island to make his TT debut, having ridden in the Cookstown 100 on the Saturday. Joey entered Lightweight, Junior, Senior and the Classic races - the latter was not actually a race for Classic machines but a name given to the final race of the week on the Friday in which machines from 300 - 1,000ccs could compete. It would allow machines like the 750 Yamaha and some of the F750 four-strokes a chance to compete, a move intended to liven up the field. The 500 race was still called the Senior but run now on the Wednesday, something that upset some of the purists who held that the Senior Race, held to be the 'Blue Riband' event of the week, was devalued by being run in the middle of the programme.

Joey had not chosen a particularly good year to commence his TT apprenticeship. The Isle of Man has something of a micro-climate of its own and this year 'Mona's' weather was being particularly capricious. Bad at the beginning of practice week, it actually caused cancellation of Monday evening's session and for good measure, race week's Classic event to be postponed for 24 hours. This led to many empty spaces on the grid as some competitors, like myself, could not change travel arrangements. Joey's late arrival in the Island meant that there was not even time to make a circuit of the course before going out in his first practice, a circumstance that I too experienced back in 1962. However, he encountered heavy rain and almost lost it on the fast right hander just before Ramsey Hairpin - Stella Maris. Joey remembers that year with the anecdote: 'I went out in Monday morning practice and didn't know which way the track went. I got to Ballacraine crossroads on my first lap and didn't know where to go so I stopped and waited for a rider who knew his way. I then followed an experienced man until he was out of sight, then I slowed and waited for another one and so on. That was how I completed my first ever TT lap.' But in a tribute to great friend Tom Herron, Joey acknowledges the valuable help and advice that he gave him in that first year while learning the course.

Joey was riding under number 65 in his first TT race, the Junior (350), and so he had a lot of traffic to contend with on the Rea Yamsel. He set off some 5m 20s behind the man he had diced with at Oulton Park, Charlie Williams riding a Maxton Yamaha, who was starting number one. On his first

Joey wasn't just a master of the TT course, he is pictured here at Ballabeg on the Southern 100 course.

racing lap of the Mountain circuit Joey cracked in a 'ton' from a standing start; his second lap of the five lap race was his fastest in a time of 22m 0.8s - over 102mph. For a newcomer to the circuit, that was a super start and a portent of things to come. His last lap was a little slower at just over 23m, which was sufficient to drop his average speed for the race down to just 99.83mph, missing a 'magic 100' debut. Some average!

In those days a 100mph lap, 22m.38s, was considered to be a pretty respectable performance. The 16th place finish he achieved was good enough to earn Joey the first of his Tourist Trophy Replicas; he was to go on to amass more than any other rider. There was a further accolade for him on his debut race though when three members of the Cookstown & DMCC won the Club team prize for the highest placed team; Joey, Billy Guthrie and Courtney Junk.

Now Joey did not have an entry in the Senior in the first instance but in riding number 44 he took over that of Gordon Pantell who had moved up the list to take an earlier number. In this race Joey went just a shade slower in terms of a total race time than he did in the Junior, but then he did have to make two pit stops in the six lapper and finished in 18th spot. Eighteenth place was still good enough to win him his second Replica of the week, with a race speed of 98.55mph. The race was won by yet another legendary Irish road racer and Joey's Island mentor, Tom Herron.

Tom was also to win the Lightweight (250) Race but this was one in which Joey's 250 Rea Yamaha was sidelined in favour of a ride in the afternoon's Classic Race; a four and a six lap race on the same day was something that many a racer declined. However, things did not go according to plan. After those two good performances earlier in the week, the 350 declined to complete another race over the Mountain Course and expired on the fourth lap when the crankshaft broke.

As TT debuts go, to come away with a couple of replicas could not be bad but one could hardly guess at the dramatic performance that he would achieve next year with comparatively scant race experience over the world's longest and most challenging course.

The Irish season of '76 would see Joey carry almost all before him. He made the 350 class at Mondello Park practically his own, winning every race he contested. The 500 too scored win after win on the short circuits but so as to be able to contest more classes, Joey converted Mervyn Robinson's 350 to a 250. This proved to be a very worthwhile exercise as he then placed third in the North West 200 and for good measure followed that up with seventh in the Formula 750 Race on the 350; an event won by Percy Tait on a 750 Suzuki.

That man Ray McCullough put it across Joey again on the 350 at the Killinchy 150 but then Dunlop was to go on to win the 500 with the fastest lap set at 107.27mph, still on the 350. It was Ray again at the Skerries where Joey was second in the 350 as Mervyn and Joey duelled in the Unlimited and Shellsport races where their positions alternated - in first and second.

It was back across the Irish sea for another visit to the Isle of Man, this time to the Southern 100 meeting on the Billown circuit at Castletown before going on to Jurby. Joseph had excelled himself by bringing home no less than 19 trophies. It was also notable as the day that he beat McCullough in a road race fair and square. Joey scored third in the 250, second in the 350 and unlimited races. On the second day of the two-day programme, he set his seal on the meeting by winning the Shell Invitation race and broke Ray's lap record that he had set on the previous day. On the Jurby Airfield track a couple of days later, Joey was in top form winning three out of four races to round off his most successful weeks racing so far.

Now a star of any meeting he raced at, Joey went on through the year to reel off wins and top three places at just about everywhere in Ireland. He further broadened his racing horizons with a new venture across the seas to Scotland, going first to Croft to win the 350 and 500 classes then on to East Fortune for a win in the 350. However, he had to give best to Bill Simpson in the Solo Invitation and 100 mile events.

It would be a long list that included all of Joey's wins and places in that triumphant season but among the highlights there was a triple win at Mondello in July, following up that feat with four wins a month later, a double at Kirkistown and treble at Aghadowey. The Ulster saw a best performance yet with a memorable second in the 500 race as he chased Stan Woods over the line on the works Suzuki, Joey on the 351 Yamaha.

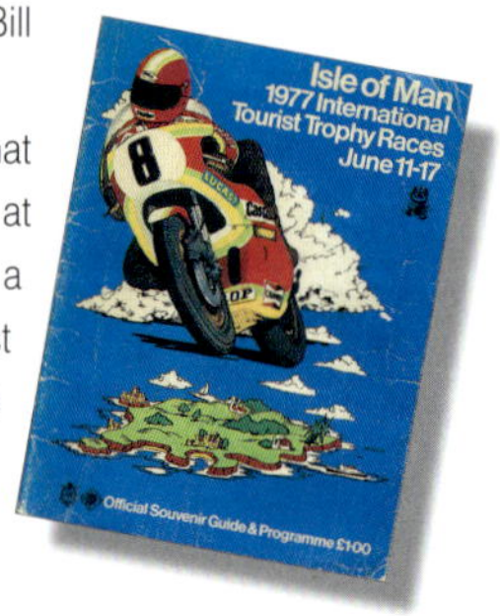

The season finished as it had progressed when Joey was awarded the trophy for Ireland's Best Road Racer of 1976. The final score of that impressive season was 30 short circuit wins and six on road circuits.

In 1977, the Rea brothers were to become ever more enthusiastic in their sponsorship of motorcycle racing. Noel and Martin were to field their own riders and John Rea became Joey's principal backer. As the Armoy Armada Newsletter of 1978 records, 'The three man team was to make the racing world sit up and take notice.'

For the new season John purchased the ex-Pat Mahoney 750 Yamaha; this had been one of the original 700cc machines that were soon upgraded to 750 as the manufacturer continued to develop them. Joey went to Oulton Park to test the bike and once it was back in the Emerald Isle, Joey quickly set to work to install the engine into a Seeley frame, the road holding of the original could certainly be improved upon. The bike was to be the spearhead of the machinery for the season, which also included a 350 cantilever sprung Yamaha and a 250 Yamsel.

Seven wins out of seven starts at Mondello and Kirkistown meetings saw Joey get off to a scintillating start to the season. It hardly seemed as though things could get any better but then twelve wins from the St.Angelo, Aghadowey and Kirkistown meetings the following month and he was beating Ray McCullough more often than the other way around. At the North West 200, Joey scored his best result in the 250 class following Tony Rutter across the line, just ahead of Ray again.

The Killinchy 150 saw the appearance of Ron Haslam on the grid and he finished second on his 500 Suzuki behind Yer Maun on his 350, but then he did go on to win the 1000 race with Joey behind Ray once more; both Ray and Joey were riding 750 Yamahas this time.

Real sponsorship came Joey's way in 1977 when the Rea brothers got seriously involved with road racing.

The TT races that year were keenly contested by works teams from Kawasaki, who fielded Mick Grant and Suzuki's trio of Charlie Williams, Steve Parrish and Pat Hennen, not to mention the best of the rest from the UK and Ireland. However, the real news that year did not concern the 'proper' racing classes but the advent of the TT Formula races, a fact that was to figure as a major factor in the future of road racing's rising star, William Joseph Dunlop. It introduced a class of racing that was to provide him with the opportunity to win world titles, an opportunity that he was to grasp so firmly that it could be described in current sporting jargon as a five year 'lockout.'

The TT Formula Races came about largely due to the Auto Cycle Union's herculean efforts to regain a world title status for the TT races. They were aided in their efforts by the fact of a diminishing availability of competitive 500cc machines to riders with which to contest Grands Prix. The TT Formula was intended to provide a class of racing which, based upon production machines, would make racing much cheaper and more available to aspiring riders and smaller manufacturers. It would eventually be a major factor, at least in racing in the UK, leading to a TT programme dominated by races for

Joey swoops down to the Bungalow in the 1977 TT aboard the Rea 750 Yamsel.

production-based machines reflected in today's Supersport classes and even Production events, in all of which Joey would feature. Indeed, it would see him on some unlikely machinery as manufacturers and dealers sought his services. It started out as a one-race World Championship but would flourish as the Formula 750 class died out and go on to be staged on both road circuits like the Ulster and tracks around Europe.

Joey was to write his name in TT records this year for a superb ride in the finale race of the week, but before doing so would polish his course knowledge by riding in three races on the 250 and 350 Rea Yamsels. The fact of Joey finishing in tenth place on the 250 in Monday's Junior Race, hardly presaged the performance to come, but when considering the names of the men that did finish in front of him, it could hardly be bad; names like winner Charlie Williams, Ian Richards, Tom Herron, Alex George, Stan Woods, Eddie Roberts, Mick Grant, Clive Horton and Joe Lindsay. Joey was to win his first of four Silver Replicas of the week in that three lapper in which he averaged just less than 95mph.

The 350 was wheeled out for the Senior Race, in fact 350's predominated in the 76-man field; indeed the only real alternative was the 500 Suzuki, one of which Phil Read raced to the top rostrum position. From his number 30 starting position and 2m 20s behind first man away Jack Findlay, Joey started the scheduled six lap race, which subsequently became five as visibility came down over the mountain and curtailed the race. Clocking 21m 58s for a standing start lap at 103mph, Joey pushed that up to 105mph on the second for his fastest lap of the race. He finished in fourth behind Tom Herron, in second was Roberts; the average speed was 103.1mph. It was a good result by anybody's calculations.

Joey was clearly learning more about the course with every race and upped his race average in the Classic event to 105mph testifying to this fact, in spite of which he only finished in 7th place. Breaking into the '20 minute club' for the first time with a lap at 108mph on the second lap, was a portent of things to come. However, that seventh place was on the day when Mick Grant, riding the 750 Kawasaki, was putting together a record breaking race average at over 110mph and new lap record at 112mph to win the day.

So we come to the day when Joey began a TT role of honour that will probably never be beaten, with his first win over the Mountain Course. The race bore the title of Schweppes Jubilee Race, event nine and open to machines up to 1,000cc. Joey started on number six in a race run to only four laps and, it has to be said, of not full International status, being what was billed as a Restricted Invitation race. All that served to achieve was the elimination of the works machinery and it presented Joey with his big chance.

For this one, Joey rode the 750 Rea Yamaha, on which he promptly distanced himself from the opposition by putting in a faster lap than the rest at 20m 25.8s, which is over 110mph - and from a standing start. His second was just 1.4 faster and at almost 111mph, was the fastest lap of the race. By comparison, Dunlop

cruised the last two laps, he even had time to stop in Ramsey Square on the last lap to check on tyre wear; this was because the race being of a National grading, only permitted the use of treaded boots. The win goes into the record books as an average speed of 108.86. As something of a footnote, it was future World Superbike Champion Carl's Dad, George Fogarty, who finished in second place on a 738cc Suzuki.

Joey was now to contest the F750 World Championship round at Brands Hatch. This Championship derived from the States. And like Formula TT, was supposed to provide an arena in which heavily modified, and available, production-based machines, would provide a cheaper - well, less expensive, class of racing up to 750ccs. The Yamaha 750 four promptly rendered machines like the Suzuki and Kawasaki triples obsolete and the class didn't last for very long.

In two legs, the Brands Hatch results bring back memories of Steve Baker, Mick Grant and Christian Sarron, with most of the field on 750's as Joey rode his 350 into 11th place and retired in the second. Haslam won the Support race as Joey finished fifth. Travelling to Aintree, Donington, Scarborough and Oulton Park that year, Joe was truly getting the flavour of International competition with the calibre of riders like Hennan, Sheene, Woods, Marshall, Potter and Haslam.

If that TT win was the highlight of the year, his Irish campaign was hardly less successful. The numbers are impressive; 33 race wins, 16 seconds and five third places. For those who may have thought that Joey Dunlop was only a master on high-speed road circuits, he finished the season with three short circuit championships - 250, 350 and 750. A plethora of accolades came his way in that most successful year; Embassy Champion, King of Kirkistown where he won five races out of five in the one day, Ace of Aghadowey, Sunflower Champion, Skerries Shellsport Champion and Southern 100 Champion.

Joey's appearance on a grid in Ireland was by now sufficient to ensure a growing and very enthusiastic crowd of Dunlop supporters. The foundations of the legend were firmly laid. Somewhere around this period his fans came up with the name of 'The Gurk,' which antecedents are from medieval times - and 'transliterates' from old Irish as 'Dark Knight.' These

Joey aboard a Rea Racing 350 Yamsel pushing the rear tyre to the limit and the fairing skimming across the tarmac.

days were also those of competition between two 'camps' of supporters, the Armoy Armada of Joey, Frank, Mervyn and Jim and the Dromara Destroyers, who were Ray McCullough, Brian Reid and Trevor Steele. The battles between the teams must have boosted the profits of the drinks companies significantly as the social side of racing both before and after competition in those days was legendary and riders would support their supporters until the early hours!

Ray McCullough, one of the most respected of Irish road racers and the man to beat for nearly two decades comments:

'It was in 1976 that I remember, the first time that he beat me, on a 350 Yamaha at Cookstown. Then there was the first time that I rode a 750. It was at the Temple. Joey had one and we raced neck and neck all the way through the race and then last time around at the hairpin and Joey was trying so hard that he overshot and I won that one. He is a true gentleman. I've never heard anyone say a bad word about him. After his big crash at Brands Hatch in 1989 he came back to just ride around in the middle of the pack working to get back on the pace. There aren't many people who could do that. He has just got to be the best road racer in the world.'

Girling

Racing at Daytona

into GPs and F750

1978-1979

Just to prove the point that he could ride any machine, he finished fifth in the 1978 Formula II race aboard a 550 Benelli.

For Joey's tenth year of racing, John Rea purchased two new Yamaha's; 350 and 750. This was also the year that Sam Taggart joined the Dunlop sponsors club by providing a 250 and Hector Neill would come up with the 500 Suzuki. Joey was now armed with the best machinery that could be bought by a privateer team, and so equipped, crossed 'the pond' to race at Daytona Beach, Florida, some five years after I did the same thing. Daytona was fast becoming the season opener for top European racers blowing away winter cobwebs.

In the April issue of the long defunct 'All Ireland Motorcycle,' there was a brief account of the meeting and headed, 'as seen by Joey Dunlop and related by Derek Mason.' From it, one learns that Sam's 250 carried Joey to a most creditable eighth place in a race won by Greg Hansford on the works Kawasaki with 'wild child' Randy Mamola on a Yamaha splitting the factory pair as Anton Mang came home third on the other in-line twin. It was a performance that went largely unnoticed and it was in spite of handling difficulties. Joey quickly discovered that Daytona is as rough as Kirkistown. The Yanks had a solution that alleviated the problem, wider rims and harder tyres. While Joey identified the answer to the problem, the necessary rims were just not available so he had to live with an ill-handling machine, something of a high-speed wrestling match in fact. If one wonders how Joey found himself in that situation, the story by Derek Mason supplies the answers. Both the bikes were new and had been run in Japan before Joey took delivery. But, Joey had suffered a bout of flu just before the bikes arrived and there had been no time at all to test and sort them. So they arrived in Daytona untested and up against top class international competition. Yer Maun was handicapped from the start.

So the 250 race proved beyond doubt, if indeed it needed to be so, that Joey could run with the best and hardest men in the business at that stage in his career, and with a new and somewhat problematical bike. Things did not go so well with the 750 Yamaha though, which is where long time mechanic Andy Inglish takes up the story. 'The Americans had decided that 750's were just getting too fast and therefore brought out a rule that required the fitting of restrictor plates in the induction tracts to 'choke' the motors and so reduce power. Willie (Dunlop) and

I fitted them but the bike never ran properly. Joey always said that there was a high speed misfire and we put it down to ignition. We borrowed another complete ignition set and chased what we took to be sparks problems throughout the week. It was very frustrating but it has to be said that we just didn't have the experience of that sort of thing in those days.' In fact, the OW 750 had holed a piston in the second practice session. This led to some hurried fettling before qualifying and there was just time for five bedding-in laps before the race in which to qualify, which was why he started in 40th place in what were described as 'turbulent conditions.' There were 80 accepted for the race, which put him at the back of the 'first wave': the field is split into two halves and has a staggered start to let the traffic thin out, a system rather like that currently used in meetings like the North West 200.

At the start of the race, Joey was caught out with a 'bogged' motor and rapidly went to the back of the pack. Nevertheless, some 30 laps into the race, Joey had coaxed his under-par Yamaha into a top 20 place. However, the misfiring was doing the motor no good at all and it eventually seized a piston. 'But the man rode like a demon in spite of all that and was slipstreaming around the big banking to make up for it', Andy said. But the report by Mason gave the reason for the retirement as broken cylinder head studs. It's worth noting too that as far as Joey could find out, every Yamaha that retired did so with the same ailment.

After the debut in the US of A, the next time out for The Man, was the Brands Hatch Easter meeting. Riding in the support races of the Transatlantic Series, luck was still running against him, as he crashed the 350 and was 'not feeling so good' and finished but 21st in the 750 race. In the Sunday's races in the three-round series: 'I knew something was wrong on the warming up lap on the 250, a soft tyre.' The reason for this was something he found out later and was caused by the tyre degrading during the transatlantic flight as the altitude affected the rubber. Rapidly fitting the wheel from the 350, which turned out to be slightly bent from the crash and in spite of that, a 16th place finish was much better than most would manage under the circumstances. Nevertheless, as Joey saw it, 'a seventh in the 750 race (won by Barry Ditchburn) could not be that bad.'

Joey, always at home on a 250, heads Bill Ingham (12) in the 1979 Lightweight TT.

Joey's first TT Honda ride in 1978 aboard a Devimead machine. It was Hailwood's come-back ride - no wonder Joey looked in pensive mood!

It was back to the familiar Irish 'push and shove' now for a couple of meetings and with another four wins under his belt, Team Dunlop made the trek down to the South of France to circuit Paul Riccard in April to contest the F750 Race. The result wasn't auspicious; 15th in an event won by Johnny Cecotto, chased home by Kenny Roberts and Steve Baker and a formidable supporting cast that filled the places in between.

May was a busy month, opening with a clean sweep of four wins at Kirkistown and a 350 win at Cookstown, though Graham Young beat him into second place, both on 350's riding in the 500 race. However, at the following Killinchy 150, Joey rode a 500 Suzuki for the first time as Hector Neill joined the band of Dunlop sponsors and this was to have long term implications. The result was a fourth place with another on the 250 and a win on the 350. Back to mainland UK for the Brands International saw Joe score top rostrum on the 250 ahead of Clive Padgett. The 750 hadn't behaved itself in practice. Joey's F750 contender had 'blown its top' somewhat terminally.

The TT in the year of '78 was the year of Mike the Bike's great comeback, and of Ron Haslam's TT debut. Mick Grant fielded the works Kawasaki and Phil Read was back again on the works Formula Hondas. For Joey, it was a landmark year in that it was his first ride in Formula races; a Devimead 812 Honda in the F1 and of all things, a 550 Benelli in the FII. The programme for that year shows that Joey took over the Benelli ride from Snuffy Davis, entered by Baron Cycle-Ops.

The race programme opened on the Saturday afternoon at 16.00 with the Formula 1 Race. Joey was riding number two on the Dave Mason entered 812 Honda; a bored out 750. He was alongside Phil Read on the Honda Britain's bigger bore 888cc bike and there were some real hard chargers on later numbers; Mike and John Williams were but two. It was a race that stays in the memories of TT aficionados as the day when Mike on the Ducati, blew away 'bad boy Read' on the works Honda. For Joey though, making his race debut on a roadster derived racer, things did not progress quite so rapidly as he would have wished. With an opening lap in 22m 17s, like Read, Joey only completed four of the scheduled six laps.

In Monday's Senior race, Joey was entered on the 350 Rea Yamaha but he subsequently switched to the 500 Suzuki which, incorrectly jetted, proved not to be a good idea as it managed just one lap at 102mph before retiring. Meanwhile, Tom Herron had been quite majestic in winning by a clear margin from Billy Guthrie. Hector Neill had bought the 500 from Billy after his debut on the bike at the '77 TT when the engine had broken its somewhat fragile connecting rods. For the Lightweight Race, Joey started number 14, ten seconds behind Hailwood and both on Yamahas; indeed they finished 11th and 12th respectively, with Joey getting in front on the first lap. Though neither were on race winning pace it should be said that Joey added another Silver Rep' to his trophy cabinet.

Getting the front wheel of the Rea Yamaha airborne – mechanical failure again spurned his chances in the Schweppes Classic.

If the Formula II Benelli 550 seemed an unlikely racing machine, it actually gained Joey a fifth place result. He came rapidly through the field from 19th on the grid to finish just behind Ron Haslam to win one more Silver replica; Joey could hardly have guessed that it would be his best placing of the week. The final race of the programme was Friday's Schweppes Classic, for machines to a 1000ccs. For this one, Joey had top billing; he started on the number one spot on the Rea 750. Joey put in a lap just short of 109mph from a standing start, which was good enough to earn fourth spot behind Grant's Kawasaki, John Williams on the 500 Suzuki and Alex George - 750 Yamaha; Phil Read was ten seconds behind on the 998 Honda Britain entry. However, he had to stop at Greeba on lap two to check on an exhaust that was disintegrating and after touring back to the pits, Joey retired as they were unable to effect any repair to the broken pipe.

Instead of a 'laundry list' of top places won by Joey throughout the rest of the Irish season, particular highlights worth noting were that Jim Dunlop appears in fourth place in the Skerries results, and it was Mervyn who won that Unlimited event with Joey second. Also, just for once, Joey didn't clean up at Aghadowey after the TT as Jack Wilkin won the 500 Race, with Joey second and Jim third. At the Ulster, Tom Herron continued on the crest of a wave by winning the big race as Joey slotted into eighth and made sixth in the 350 won by Jon Ekerold. Others who managed to put it across 'our man' as he racked up a further dozen wins, were Noel Hudson at Carrowdore and Aghadowey, Con Law, Conor McGinn and Austin Kinsella at Mondello.

Phil Read got away first in the 1978 TT. It wasn't Joey's day – he broke down on the fourth lap. Roger Nichols carried the number three.

Joey, of course didn't win everything but it is a commentary of his winning form that the occasions when he didn't win are recorded here.

Now with a decade of racing behind him, for 1979 Joey was on the verge of greater things and a season when he would really put himself about on the Continent and his progress would be noticed by at least one works team. Starting the '79 season, with another tilt at the Daytona banking with a new 750 Yamaha, they got no nearer getting the bike to run properly with its restrictors and after a somewhat troubled practice is shown as finishing in 74th place, due to having broken its crankshaft early in the race. The 250 race though was much better as Joey came in 12th in the event in which Skip Aksland beat Freddie Spencer to the top spot.

In France and back on the Paul Riccard circuit, the 750 Yamaha seized a piston but on the 250, eleventh was a reasonable result in a top class field. Worth noting was the fact that this was in front of Graeme McGregor, a man who would figure largely in his career a year later. On to Mettet in Belgium, Joey finished in seventh place in a 500 event. But a new venture for him was when he returned to the UK at the Oulton short circuit where Ron Haslam took a double and Jim beat Joey for second in the 250; then, scoring 6th on the 750 was the end result of a fierce battle at the front of the field.

Suzuki-mounted Dunlop pictured during the 1979 TT. Sadly, he retired on the second lap; Hailwood went on to win the race on a similar machine.

It was business as usual on the Irish racing scene with more wins and scraps with Ray McCullough on the run up to what was to be a most memorable North West 200 for three reasons. Two of those were Joey's first wins on the dramatically fast road circuit. That year, Dunlop won not only the Match Race as part of Tom Herron's Team, but came first in the 1000 Race after a tremendous dice with Roger Marshall and to grab the win by just half a bike's length at the flag. For good measure, he also finished fifth in the 350 and 500 races. Later in the day, he switched to the 750 Rea Yamaha for the 1000 race. Among the opposition were Mick Grant and Ron Haslam and Graeme Crosby but on the day they were all helpless against the brilliant Dunlop.

That meeting was a tragedy for several reasons and all affecting Joey and his family deeply. It was Tom Herron's last NW 200 as he crashed fatally during the last race when he was chasing Steve Parrish. He sustained severe chest injuries from which he died. Tom was a very good friend of Joey but as if that were not bad enough, Frank Kennedy also crashed with the same end result. Frank had been a great companion through Joey's career and this hit the Dunlops really hard. The news of his death was a great shock to all the Irish fans that day as Tom was at the top of his career and a very popular public figure as well as in the paddock..

In the year of '79 the Isle of Man races were billed as the Millennium TT; a 1000 years of independent government in the Isle of Man. But for Joey it was no better than the previous year. The TT Formula I World Championship Race saw Joey with a most unfamiliar mount; a Benelli Sei - an 896cc six cylinder, Italy's answer to the Honda six. Last year's FII result had obviously encouraged the British Importers, Agrati, to become more involved but it has to be said that the somewhat unwieldy Benelli was as near a production bike as made little difference and Joey was never to be a fan of production class machines with their treaded tyres and wayward navigational qualities. He completed just one lap at 24.15 before retiring; and as a personal note, I fell off a standard Honda CB900 at Govenors Bridge, got back on and finished 22nd.

Next came the Senior Race in which Joey was riding Hector Neill's 496 Suzuki 'square four,' the standard kit for serious 500 class racers.

A slippery Quarter Bridge held no fears for Joey during this practice shot in 1979 aboard Hector Neil's RG 500. He was a master in the wet but saw no sense in getting wet, hence the rather fetching wet suit!

After the failure of his Yamahas last year, Mike Hailwood was similarly kitted from Suzuki GB and just decimated the opposition, setting new lap and race records on his way to the top podium position. But this race was not to do much to build the reputation of the man who would eventually become the most successful TT racer ever; for him, just a two-lap race. The first at 20m.56s would have placed Joe in eighth place but then a slow lap and back to the pits.

The Junior 250 race was not to do much for the Dunlop reputation either. He completed only five of the scheduled six laps and was never really in amongst the top runners before retiring. Come the FII Race and Joey again fielded the Benelli, this time listed as a 597, so some tuning had taken place. However, all that proved was that the standard setup was better, as his lap times were not as good as the previous year and he even finished out of the Replicas; this event was recorded by the author as one in which superior machinery got him home in eighth, in front of Joey in 13th.

And so to the Schweppes Classic Race, one celebrated for the fact that Alex George and Mike the Bike duelled all the way through; a 1000cc four stroke FI against the 500 stroker. Seconds apart throughout the entire race - it was won by Alex, just a memorable 2.6 seconds in front. Meanwhile, the 750 Rea Yamaha carried Joey to sixth place; from his starting number of 38 he scored a 108.96mph average and missed a 110mph lap by just a second.

Back home again and the Killinchy 150 of that year was notable for the fact that not only did Dunlop score a triple win but also in each race he set new records for the class; 250, 350 and 1000. Another four wins at Aghadowey, four more at Kirkistown and Joey's wins were becoming quite the rule and indeed it was only Donny Robinson who was able to take a race from him in the 350 event.

The Southern 100 races held on the Billown circuit on the Isle of Man, has many similarities to some Irish road circuits in the humps and bumps and blind bends and on it Joey was to score some notable victories through the next two decades. This year he was on top form to take the flag first three times out of four; George Fogarty took the other one. Then on to a Dunlop milestone as he competed in the British Grand Prix at Silverstone in July on his 350, placing 15th. At Le Mans for the 'French' and Joey made 9th place. An International win on the 750 followed at Zeltweg in Austria before returning to the F750 Championship Series; Assen, Hockenheim and Rijeka.

Among the many stories that I collected from many of Joey's friends was this one which might well have taken place this year but I've been unable to pin it down exactly. Before departing for one of his races behind the then 'iron curtain', Joey's ancient Bedford van had seemed to him at the last moment to be rattling rather more than usual. With some prescience, he had tucked a spare crankshaft he happened to have under the seat, 'just in case.' Sure enough, miles from nowhere in the foothills of goodness knows where, the Bedford ground to a halt. Joey then set to and changed the crank by the side of the road. With this sort of self acquired mechanical ability, it becomes easy to understand that fettling a race bike out of the back of a van is almost second nature.

Holland wasn't so good as he placed 17th and 16th, a little better in Germany with 9th in the first leg but then retired with a blown engine in the second; Joey was suffering from detonation problems and the bike was never really performing. In Yugoslavia an 11th and another retirement were all recompense for the hours of driving around the Continent. A return to the UK for the Race of the Year and in '79 it was held at Oulton Park in September. It was the scene of a duel between Barry Sheene on the 680 Suzuki against a Kenny Roberts on top form who took the win; Joey finished in tenth place.

Joey continued to dominate the Irish road-racing scene winning again and again. On to the Ulster of that year it was only Donny Robinson, once more, who could deny him a win, pushing him into second in the 350 event. On the Suzuki, Joe collected the scalps of John Newbold in the 500 race and Roger Marshall in the 1000.

A quick stocktaking of Dunlop's performances through years 1974 to '79, records 115 short circuit victories and add to this 46 road circuit wins. Dunlop had surely arrived and Suzuki's Race Team Manager, Rex White, was just one who had noticed his rise in stature as a rider.

1979 was the year of the production of the now famous, and still on Duke video lists, 'The Road Racers.' It features Joey, Mervyn and another neighbour, Frank. Quoting from *'RPM'* May '95, 'as members of the so-called Armoy Armada, they brought a new dimension to competitive road racing, in their battles with Ray McCullough, Brian Ried and Trevor Steele, the Dromara Destroyers. The mostly good-natured banter between their

Sam Taggart joined the Dunlop sponsors club in 1979 and provided him with a 250 Yamaha. Joey is pictured during a TT practice lap.

respective bands of supporters, off the track, and the white-hot battles on it, epitomised the golden era of Irish road racing.' Harold Crooks, writing in the same issue, remembers one of Joey's comments after what he referred to as an incredible 350 race in 1977 with Ray McCullough at the Temple 100: 'I have never ridden like that before, or been involved in such madness before. But one thing is for sure, I will never do it again.' Given Joey's phlegmatic nature, it does reveal how intense was the competition in the late '70s on the roads of Ireland.

DAF Trucks

The Wanted Man

works rider for Suzuki and Honda 1980-81

Joey's 1980 season started in Daytona where he would have one more tilt at the awesome banking, at least it seemed that way to me back in 1973. In the 200 Mile Experts Race, 'Team Joe' came no nearer to getting the 750 sorted as Dunlop retired but was officially classified as finishing in 66th place. In the 100 Mile 250 event won by Eddie Lawson with Anton Mang and Freddie Spencer in attendance, Joey was placed 20th. The world class entry was a reflection of growing interest in the event by manufacturers and the availability of works machinery to well-sponsored teams.

Perhaps curiously, the Irish season had not opened with Joey exhibiting his usual dominance at the local circuits. There were, of course, many good places but it was in fact not until the Leinster 200 meeting at Mondello in May that Joe actually scored a first; this on the 350.

The familiar yellow helmet took on a black line for this shot during evening practice at Greeba Castle.

This year's North West 200 was to become indelibly imprinted upon Joey's memory with the death of Mervyn (Robo) Robinson. His near- neighbour, great friend, and eventual brother-in-law, Mervyn had encouraged a schoolboy Dunlop to take an interest in his own racing and was to become something of a mentor. With Frank being killed the previous year, this latest blow was to cause Dunlop to seriously consider giving up the sport.

Joey's first race in the TT in 1980 was the Senior; no foray into Formula racing this year. Riding Number 5 and listed as on a 498 Yamaha, Joey in fact wheeled out his trusty 350 and started on the grid alongside Steve Cull, mounted on a 500 Suzuki. Graeme Crosby won the race from Steve Cull and Joey's average of 106.79mph earned him a Silver Replica, the first of three he'd win that week. Prize money for that was shown in the results as £240. Joey, by being placed 12th in the Junior race on the 250 earned himself £50 in prize money that could hardly have paid for the fuel it used during the TT, a poor reward indeed. But it was still worth a 'Bronze.'

The Classic Race was the first time that Joey rode bearing his now famous racing Number 3 on the 750 Rea-Yamaha. And it's easy to see why he requests that number after this momentous result and the way he won, beating the combined might of works Hondas, ridden by Mick Grant and Ron Haslam. Haslam was riding 8 and Grant 12, but Joey had got his race face on and on the standing start lap he took 17.6 seconds out of Mick Grant's 1062 RSC Honda. With his vast experience of the Mountain circuit,

Final adjustments amid the smoke on the start line in 1980.

Grant was thought to be the 'man most likely to' and was bearing Honda's great expectations; with Haslam riding 'shotgun'. That, however, neglects Graeme McGregor on a 998 FI Honda who in fact put in a lap at 20.22 to briefly run second before retiring. It looked as though Joey was on the crest of a wave but only he knew at that stage that the petrol tank-retaining strap had broken. While it was hardly likely to fly off, over the bumps and jumps, it required Joey to brace it in place with his knees, and there is quite enough to do racing the Mountain circuit without that distraction!

There's a story behind that petrol tank and Joey's race tactics. Hector Neill has vivid memories of this race and the boost that it gave to Joey's career. He and Joey had hatched a plot in which a spare tank was borrowed from Sam McClements and Hector had taken it into Douglas to have the bottom cut out and an extra inch added to increase the capacity to something like the permitted maximum by the regulations; 32 litres. And Joey said in interview after the race; 'That extra inch meant that I could make just the one pit stop.' In a later interview he recorded that 'we fooled them by making just that one stop.'

Joey completely off the ground at Ballacrye Leap on his 350 Rea Racing Yamaha on a flat out top gear section of the TT course.

As a backdrop, the day before that race, Hector had been having a meal with Rex White and Suzuki Chief Mechanic Martyn Ogborne. 'So who will win tomorrow then,' Rex asked Hector. To which he responded, 'The wee fellow called Joey Dunlop.' Well, they didn't really believe him and after some further chat on the subject, Hector threw down the gauntlet by challenging them to give Joey a ride if he really did win.

So while Joey was coping with the broken strap, he was also carrying much more fuel - and weight. Nevertheless, Joey lapped ever faster on his second lap circulating in 19.53 against Grant's 20.00.6. At the end of the second lap Joey led Grant by 25 seconds, though Mick actually pulled back four seconds on the third lap as Joey came into to refuel.

Now in that race it was possible to use 'dump fillers' and naturally Honda team Manager Barry Symmons used that to advantage to dump a full tank of fuel in seconds into Mick's tank and he departed in haste having taken back half a minute out of Joey's lead. He had sat in the pits carefully concealing the broken tank strap with his legs from the scrutineers who would probably have prevented him continuing, while the pit crew 'dribbled' all that extra fuel in through the filler provided by the organisers. Joey's lead was now down to just 2.9 seconds and to the thousands listening to the radio around the course, the race suddenly came alive.

Joey knew the score from his signalling boards around the course and having used some of the extra fuel and top weight that he was carrying, put in a blistering lap on the fifth. He was seven seconds faster than Mick who was obviously doing his damnedest but on the day that wasn't enough. Grant, it seemed, could urge the big Honda on no faster and on his last lap circulated in 19.59, five seconds longer than his fifth. But Joe was riding like a man on a mission on the last lap of that memorable race, smashing the lap record and leaving it at 19m 38.8s; a speed of 115.22mph. He won by half a minute and his performance had not gone unnoticed by Barry Symmons.

Barry, commenting on that ride: 'We had got Mick Grant refuelled with a quick filler in around four seconds - and away. Then we watched Joey come in on the Rea 750 with the loose tank; take 53 seconds to fill up using the standard fillers and still go on to beat Mick. After watching that performance, I knew that he was the man to beat in the Island. We just had to have him.'

Parliament Square, Ramsey aboard the Rea 350 Yamaha in 1980.

As if to hammer home that thought, next came the Ulster Grand Prix. The Honda and Suzuki factories represented by their UK operations were at it hammer and tongs in their attempts to win the Formula 1 World Championship. Graeme Crosby was Suzuki's front runner and had his FI TT win under his belt, so a win in the class at the Ulster could clinch the title if only Honda didn't score too many points in the places.

It was up to Joe to finish in front of the Hondas and assist Graeme all he could; i.e., let him win. The result of that race went down in history as reported by Jimmy Walker in the August 8th issue of the *Belfast Telegraph* supplement on the race. 'It was embarrassing for the title contender, when Joey, after having scorched off into a commanding lead, eased off on the last lap to let him by and hand him the championship on a plate'. Before Joey eased the strain on the throttle wire, he set a new lap record at 118.92mph. He was now clearly hot property as a top rider and Symmons and Rex White both wanted his signature for 1981.

Joey accepts the congratulations of everyone in the press centre after his win in 1980.

There was a further piece of the jigsaw that fell into place before contracts were signed for the coming season that would make Joey a full-time team member of a UK manufacturer's team. While Barry was prime mover in signing up Joey for Honda, the initial impetus came really from John Rea. At the Ulster in '77, John Rea invited Barry back to his bungalow for a chat after the race. Barry well remembers being cornered between the fridge and washing machine in the kitchen for two and a half-hours while John almost convinced him there and then that Honda really had to have him.

him. After that TT he was actually preaching to the converted anyway. To set the seal on a bandwagon that was already starting to roll, it was John who got David Wood to ring Barry later in '79 to get negotiations started to get Joey to sign for Honda at a stage when Suzuki were already planning to do likewise. It would be a historical contract, one that started an association that would outlast that of any other rider in racing history.

Winners of the classic race in 1980. On his faithful Rea Yamaha, Joey saw off the opposition of Honda riders Mick Grant, second, and Ron Haslam, third.

Recording those momentous events in Joey's 1980 season, neglects the Irish season in which some 14 wins came his way and included several Man of the Meeting titles for winning the big race of the day, plus a double at the Southern 100 races. Then there was a treble win at the Mondello Park Race of the Year, another triple win at Kirkistown, polished off with a double at Aghadowey.

Rex White, Team Manager of Suzuki GB at the time, recalls memories of Joey in 1980 from the rides that Dunlop rode for him as part of the Suzuki GB Race Team that year. 'Joey wasn't a team man. He was unique; his own man entirely. We had been aware of Joey from his brilliant riding of Hector Neill's Suzuki 500 at Dundrod, during 1979 and knew that at the Ulster he was unbeatable. Graeme Crosby was chasing the FI World Championship at the time and we needed to get him some backup to combat the effort that Honda were putting into their bid for the title. We naturally wanted Crosby to win for us and if Joey could finish in front of the Hondas, Haslam in particular, we could win. So I made Joey an offer that he accepted straight away, he didn't haggle, and he had his first ride for us at Silverstone. We rated him as superb on road circuits, so when he finished second there I though it was a really good effort. John Newbold finished third and Ron was pushed back to fourth, which was very good for Suzuki and a tribute to Joey's ability to switch to a big four-stroke, and on a track at that.'

He went on: 'Joey also scored second to Croz at Donington in the Forward Trust FI Race and this time kept Mick Grant's Honda in third. Then there was Cadwell Park where Joey was ninth as Graeme won again, but when it came to the Ulster World Championship Race, this is the one that people remember. It was the day that Joey just disappeared away in front and then towards the end

end of the race started to slow up to wait for Crosby. The trouble was, that this allowed Haslam to get past and take the lead but then he slid off at the Hairpin and Joey just shadowed Graeme across the line and it was that really that allowed Crosby to win the Championship. It was a terrific effort and afterwards that I made Joey an offer to ride for us next year as Croz was going on to the Grands Prix. However, he didn't respond as I suppose

The start of Joey's first year with Honda in 1981. He is pictured at Governors Bridge. It was to be the beginning of a unique partnership.

Honda made him a better offer, but I think John Rea had some influence there. Joey's an interesting character with a heart of gold.'

So Joey had signed up for the Honda Team for 1981. It meant several things would change for The Man. From living in a small town in Northern Ireland it would require him to move to most unfamiliar surroundings, a flat near Honda's Chiswick (London) headquarters. It also meant that he would have to learn to work with mechanics who would do all the preparation on the bikes that he would ride; and Joey had for so many years prepared his own machinery that he would find this a tough one to get used to. Then there was publicity and promotional events in which he would be involved in and that would be anathema to the quiet family man from Ballymoney.

Team Manager Symmons has an anecdote in mind of the time just after Joey had placed his signature on the contract. It made Barry realise that the man had hidden depths when Joey, during the following conversation about team conditions, interjected pointedly saying that, 'he did not want any of them girls.' Barry was completely nonplussed and asked what girls he meant. 'Them on the stands (at the shows) without proper clothes on', Joe retorted. 'Well we weren't actually going to give you one anyway,' responded Barry, jocularly. And while after the event, he was sure that Joey had a twinkle in his eye when he said that, he still believes that Dunlop was making a point. 'The man is as true and honest as any man I know,' was how Barry describes him.

Three of the greats, Alex George, Ron Haslam and Joey, all in happy mood despite Hondas black protest following the events of the Formula One race in 1981.

Joey's first year with Honda has been variously described by those who were enthusiastic about his career as nondescript, in fact 'totally forgettable' in the Belfast Telegraph. But given his almost alien environment and the absence of regularly honing his riding skills on the roads of Ireland, that season's results did not really fit that description though Symmons did grow to appreciate how Dunlop's unhappiness was carefully concealed behind the man's reserved, phlegmatic character.

Motor Cycle News had launched the Street Bike Championship for road bikes that year and Honda were fielding their newly launched CB1100 roadster in the Championship. Joey, as a team member would have to pilot what must have been to him, a somewhat unwieldy beast; though as hardened production class man, I found at the time that they set new standards for the class. Nevertheless, at March's Donington Park opener, Joey was only beaten by team mate Ron Haslam with Lennart Backstrom third on a Laverda and Mick Grant fourth on a Suzuki. It was hardly an inauspicious debut in production racing, a class that he would never really like but would nevertheless provide him with a win at the Ulster Grand Prix some years later.

At that same meeting, while sixth in the ITV World of Sport Race was nothing to write home about, it's worth noting that winner Sheene's GP Yamaha was chased home by Croz on a similar Suzuki and Kork Ballington on Kawasaki's GP contender. Then came Keith Heuwen on another Suzy and Haslam and Joey on the big and probably outgunned and out-handled FI bikes.

True, the following Cadwell Park meeting was quite unremarkable with a seventh place for Joey, but even that was still chasing home the other works riders. The three-meeting, six-race Marlborough Transatlantic Match Races, however, are best forgotten by Dunlop fans. Randy Mamola won both Brands legs on Good Friday as Joey made 10th and 13th. At Mallory

The Formula I race was won by works Suzuki rider Graeme Crosby. His controversial victory following a start line debacle, ended in the Black Friday Protest. Ron Haslam and Joey, second and third respectively, acknowledge the crowds.

on Sunday, Ron Haslam grabbed the first race with Joey 12th, improving by one place in the second as Randy made it three wins. Oulton Park on Monday was Sheene's turn to win while Joey chased Ron home for ninth. The last leg of the series was sensationally won by Dave Potter, ahead of Freddie Spencer. Dunlop followed Roger Marshall over the line for his best result in the series - seventh.

It was back to the roads of Ireland for the North West once more. Even if 'Yer Maun' was not a happy team member, the fact of being on familiar ground and among fans, revitalised him to top form, to the extent that he set a new lap record, positively blitzing the field on his 1123 cc Honda and top spot on the rostrum. A week later at Killinchy, he repeated the performance. The old spark still burned brightly.

The Isle of Man Tourist Trophy Races of 1981 were the scene of a remarkable public protest by the manufacturer that has given more support to the famous races than any other; Honda. The protest was commonly referred to as 'Black Friday.' It was the day when Honda's team turned up on the grid for the Classic Race, all wearing black leathers. This was to make the point that in their view, a ruling by the meeting's stewards regarding Honda's protest in the FI Race against Graeme Crosby, seemed to them to have cost Honda the race.

Graeme, on his Suzuki, had finished in front of Ron Haslam - on time, and there's the rub. Graeme had not been ready to start his race from the appointed number 16 and was still changing wheels. He was allowed to start from the back of the grid, by which time the Honda Team of Joey, Alex George and Ron Haslam were all on their merry way. Joey put up the fastest first lap at 20.04 and Crosby taking almost 23 seconds longer as he charged through the traffic from his late starting position. As the race developed, so did some initial confusion as to whether the timekeepers had made adjustments to their calculations, either resetting Crosby's time from his new starting position, or whether the clocks were effectively running from the time that he should have started.

'Simmo's' recollections from that time are that Honda had information that Crosby had lost the time and therefore allowed their men to run at speeds that they were comfortable with. Joey put

Joey put in a 20.06 lap, with Mick Grant, now a Suzuki Team member, actually pulling back a few seconds, but Croz taking 14 seconds longer than Joey; Grant though would not complete another lap. In the pits it now seemed that Crosby's time was to be taken from his revised starting position. Honda were already arguing against the decision as Joey was starting to slow, taking a long second pit stop which would effectively put him out of contention as Haslam came into second place and Joey was to finish third. It was the ACU's decision not to allow Honda's protest that prompted the 'Black Friday' exercise as a visible means of conveying to the tens of thousands of spectators Honda belief that the decision had cost them the race.

Joey wasn't best pleased at finishing third and for the Friday's Classic Race, outsped his fellow team members in pursuit of Crosby who had put in a fastest first lap at 19.50, leading Joey by six seconds. Grant was snapping at his heels just one second behind. Joey's second lap was to become a new lap record at over 115mph (19m.37s), in fact Croz was only fractionally slower, by just 0.8s. However, a fuelling miscalculation now put Joey out of contention and he was to retire on the fourth lap as Graeme went on to his second win of the week.

One of Team Manager Symmons' memories of that first year that Joey joined the Team is revealed in an anecdote: 'We gave Joey a Renault car for him to use; he drives the course in the dark, to use the headlights and learn the course. He came in the next day and was clearly unhappy. I eventually managed to get out of him the fact that he usually used a Ford Escort for that job. The Renault just wasn't giving the feedback and he couldn't get on with it. He wasn't a happy man. We gave him an Escort and he was right back on track.'

He recounted another little story that bares a little more of Dunlop's character. 'He was so secretive about how he set his bikes up that he would come down the pit lane after practice and reset his steering damper to zero so as not to give anything away. However, mechanic Dave Sleet caught him out by watching him set the damper when he thought nobody was around prior to going out, and counted the 'clicks' to spot the damper setting he was using. So, one day just as Joey was going out to practice, Dave ran after him to say: "Don't worry about the steering damper setting Joey, I've put it on six clicks." Joey was positively dumbfounded.'

The Honda Team swept the board in the FI Race at the British GP but as they say, in reverse order. The score read: Joey, Wayne Gardener and Ron, again at the top of his form. The Ulster that year was another where Joey's star did not shine as brightly as other years with Haslam winning the FI Race as Joey was fifth. Ron did a repeat in the Classic Race after overhauling Grant and Newbold on the way as Joey lost the battle with Gary Lingham for fourth.

With his first season as a Honda team man nearing an end, it was concluded by a first visit to Macau in company with Ron Haslam. It was Ron who won the first of the two-leg races with Joey in fifth place behind the 500 Yamahas of Boet van Dulman, Sadeao Asami and Charlie Williams. However, there's a tale behind that race as when he came into the pits after the race, Joey collapsed. 'The high temperature and high humidity had proved a little too much for him as he fought the big Honda through the Armco lined twists and turns of the infamous circuit,' explained Symmons. Joey was promptly wrapped in wet towels and given salt tablets and there was certainly no suggestion that he should go out in the second leg. It was his decision to race again and it was Asami who won this time, taking the top spot from Ron as a clearly below par Dunlop was placed seventh.

A visit to South Africa was the final event of the year. Perhaps curiously, Joey's best result was a second place in the Streetbike Race at Kyalami, and then scored 5th in the Match Race and 12th in the Superbike event. The meeting at Kyalami was a somewhat inauspicious end to the year and Joey, back at Chiswick, finally let it be known that what he needed to be a happy man, simply, was to get back home to his own people and be able to work on the bikes himself. Barry Symmons again recalls: 'In that first year that he rode for us, he came to the team as a closed book and it really wasn't working. The only thing we could do to start building confidence with him was to give him a couple of bikes and let him go his own way. The rest, as they say, is history.' And this was to set the pattern for Joey's unique relationship with Honda for the rest of his racing career.

A fabulous shot as Joey peels into Sulby Bridge in the Senior Race ahead of Jeff Sayle and Graeme McGregor.

The Champion starts his F1 reign

1982-1983

A real one-off in every sense of the word. In 1983 Joey was given a factory 998cc engine by Honda but to withstand the hammering of short circuits and road races in Ireland, a hand-made frame was crafted by top welder of the time, Mervyn Scott, pictured third from left. To cut down on weight Joey sourced some titanium bolts. Also in the picture is Jackie Grahams and David Wood.

Looking back at Joey's second year with Honda it might, perhaps uncharitably, be said that it was not such a good season from the fact that he was beaten several times on what might be termed 'his own ground.'

Barry Symmons recalls that on the occasions (particularly in Ireland) when team-mate Ron Haslam did beat Joey, he would be subjected to vociferous comment by some of his fans to the effect that Ron must have been given the better bike. 'That just wasn't true,' says Barry. 'Ron really was on top form that year.' And indeed the season's results show that Ron won most of the big races he contested. On the top of his form, he would go on to Grands Prix the following year and score rostrum places.

By some commentators' standards, Joey's performances that year may have lacked the highlights of others, but at the end of it, a first of six World Championships would be in his pocket. There were just three rounds in the FI Championship that year; The Island, Portugal and Ireland. In the TT, Ron took the win with Joey running second; at Vila Real, fellow Honda team member Wayne Gardner did the business as Joey once more scored second; and then the Ulster where he was again the bridesmaid. However, with Ron Haslam missing the Portugal round, three seconds for the top points scorer, did the job for Joey.

Joey holds as one of his best racing memories of the eighties, the day he crossed the line at the Ulster as the new World FI Champion - for the first time. As it happened, while Ron Haslam took the win in the FI race at the Ulster in the open event, Joey beat Ron this time but they were only second and third, as it was Roger Marshall who put it across both of them on the Suzuki.

Thinking through his game plan. Joey contemplates the Formula One race which he went on to win.

If Joey seems somewhat reclusive in a paddock before a race, he is anything but to fellow competitors with a problem. At the Portuguese round of the Championship, Geoff Johnson's van had gasped its last on reaching the meeting after a hard passage over the mountains, en-route from the UK to Vila Real. There was no chance of a repair but Joey came up with the solution. A quick trip to the local motorway and after unbolting a section of Armco, an impromptu tow bar was improvised by bolting his van's bumper to Geoff's, and so Joey towed Geoff's van back to the UK. And as it happened in the race, Geoff finished the third man home on his Suzuki in the FI Race, behind Joey.

So while that year did close with Joey as FI Champion, in truth, the actual results pale compared to some previous seasons. It was perhaps ironic that several race wins were in his least favourite class, Streetbike races. Perhaps the most notable was at Donington, though there were several others but they were on Irish home ground. Nevertheless, Joey certainly hadn't lost the knack of winning at Aghadowey, where the 998 Honda Special scooped three wins. Almost by way of change though, he didn't win the North West as Mick Grant won the big race with Joey but 0.02 of a second down, practically riding pillion and Rob McElnea was pushing hard right behind them.

The fabulously turned out Honda awaits the great man who is deep in conversation with a member of the Honda crew.

Honda published several Newsletters charting the progress of the Race Team during the year and in the Autumn 1993 edition, there was one paragraph that mentioned the fact that Honda had given Joey a F1 engine to use on short circuits or Irish roads. There is a story behind that cryptic revelation. The alloy chassis that housed that motor was built by Joey and Mervyn Scott, who everybody knew by the name of Curly. Joey wanted not just as light a machine as could be built but one with a longer wheel base for better handling at high speed over the bumpy Irish road circuits. Curly was counted as the best alloy welder in Ireland at that time and made a real work of art of the job. Joey was a fanatic about weight, and having built an alloy chassis would then buy the best nuts and bolts to save weight. Some of the titanium bolts on that machine and later on the John Harris 600, came via Ferry Brouwer; the Arai man. He had a contact in Russia who used to work on MIG fighter aircraft and those nuts and bolts really were the business.

Getting ready for the blast down Bray Hill during the Formula One race of 1982.

If indeed any of the season of '82 was bad - and it wasn't really, then at the 26th June meeting at Aghadowey, Joey made a clean sweep with a triple win on the special Honda. At Mondello Park he played out the Irish season with another win before flying off to the Macau Grand Prix in company with Ron and Mick Grant. Between the high walls and steel barriers of Macau, Ron won one leg of the two-race event and Mick the other, while Joey scored third and fourth.

As Joey looked forward to the 1983 season, he told *'Road Racing'* magazine reporter John Brown, about the differences between racing between the walls and hedges as opposed to short circuit tracks. 'With seven rounds of the FI Championship planned, it would leave me less time for short circuit races anyway. I can't just switch on and off at will as riders like Ron seem to be able to do. Ron and the other top short circuit lads were born and bred to that style of racing and they can get away with this style at the odd road race meeting. My style does not bring the best results at Brands Hatch or Donington, although I did win a Streetbike Round there,' said Joey. Brown went on to comment: 'There is no doubt that Dunlop is at a disadvantage because he came to the short circuits at the age of almost 30 with nothing but road racing as a background. For Joey, racing is a thing that flows and he doesn't get on with the idea of dropping a bike into a short circuit corner.You only have to compare the nearly worn out studs on the scratched knees of Haslam's leathers to the almost untouched ones on Joey's to understand the difference in style between them.'

Ron Haslam remembered some of the races that he had had with Joey on the Irish roads and indeed commented that he had really gone rather well on the Honda CB1100R in Streetbikes races. 'We had some fantastic scraps in the early days. I remember one Ulster when we were lapping around 119mph on treaded tyres and I dropped it at the Hairpin on the last lap. He really was very good on the 1100Rs. There was the time at Brands when he was pushing me very hard in the Streetbike race, he was really on the pipe that day. We came down out of Druids and it was just wet/dry and Joey lost it in a big way. I know he won a round at Donington. He was always very quiet and pleasant, a good team member. He never boasted or bragged and rather kept himself to himself; a lad on his own.'

Thinking of the association between Ron and Joey reminded me of the time I got my own call from Barry Symmons to run-in the endurance bike

It could only be Joey Dunlop. The Isle of Man was his second home and he knew every inch of the road.

Joey and Ron were to partner on in the 1000 Kilometre event at Donington. The bike was as expected, a total 'beaut' and I recorded the race test for *Motorcycle Racing* magazine. In the event, Ron and Joey were leading the race by a mile, lapping my privateer Honda like a train. As it happened, the bike 'blew' when an exhaust valve let go; my team scored 13th.

1983 was another year with lows and highs. It didn't really begin too well in the UK as Donington, Cadwell Park and Thruxton in March saw Joe languishing down in the lower places. But back on the familiar Irish circuits in April and May there were victories at Aghadowey, Tandragee and Mondello on the 'home-brew' FI bike. On the UK mainland again the Transnational Series was little better, but back on his home stamping ground at the North West, Joey did the business once more and it's worth noting that in doing so in the 500 race, it was on the new 500 three-cylinder stroker. Wheeling out the big four-stroke, Joey then grabbed top honours in the big race of the day and for good measure took third in the Superbike race to Graham Wood on a 750 Yamaha and Norman Brown on a 500 Suzuki.

The North West 200 has always been seen as the one that riders do in order to get 'set up' for the TT. So Joey might have been seen as firm favourite for the Island. But then Honda had chosen to introduce the 750 VF-based racer in preparation for the 750cc limit to be introduced for the Formula I Class the following year. Even to the maestro, while Honda had managed to increase the capacity to 850cc, it looked like a tall order

Assen, 1983 and on a blazing hot day, Joey wheelies away from the line much to the delight of a packed grandstand. He gets away ahead of Mick Grant (10), future 500cc World Champion Wayne Gardner (8) and Rob McElnea (19).

against the established 1000cc Suzukis that he would have to beat.

The fact of that 850 being a vee four was claimed by Barry Symmons to make it eminently suitable for the TT course due to the midrange torque provided by the engine configuration. However, if there were doubts, then Joey rose to the occasion and just blew the Suzukis away with a new lap record from a standing start of 19m 33.6s, a speed of 115.73mph.

A fabulous shot of Joey heeling over the big Honda during the 1983 Formula I series at Assen.

Now, with Suzuki, Mick Grant and team mate Rob McElnea just couldn't get to grips with Joey and Mick, in second place, was half a minute behind at the flag; Joey set a new race record for good measure. Roger Marshall brought the other 850 Honda into fourth place.

The Senior Classic race contained a couple of surprises for Honda though; one was Norman Brown on a Suzuki 500 who had started number one and made the fastest first lap to look as though he'd see off the big four-strokes. Joey was running second, neck and neck with Mick Grant.

A change of rubber and Joey prepares to charge off down Bray Hill.

Norman put in a scintillating second lap to break Joey's lap record and put his marker down at 116.19mph in spite of Joey going even faster himself drawing four seconds away from Mick and still in second place. But then things started to come apart as Norman's ignition system stopped supplying sparks to the 'square four' and 'big Rob' started his charge to take the lead.

As Joey slowed a little, Con Law now slipped into second place clocking the fastest time during the fourth lap. The final surprise in that race, at least for Mick Grant, was Charlie Williams riding a Yoshimura-kitted, Kawasaki-engined Harris, who overtook him to grab fourth place.

So Joey had the top score in the first of the three-round FI Championship and would next go onto the Dutch TT at Assen. Although Assen is partly a public road circuit, Joey sees it differently: 'It's just like a normal track. Give me Dundrod or the Isle of Man any time.' The result of the Dutch was in fact far better than Joey had dared hope as he placed second to Rob Mac. Not only that, he was good enough on a track he didn't really like, to lead the Honda Team home in fine style with Roger Marshall third and Wayne Gardner fourth.

The last of the series was the Ulster Grand Prix. But a damp and murky Dundrod circuit greeted the riders and Joey led the Championship by just two points. To emphasise how important Honda regarded the championship title, they really pulled a rabbit out of the hat and rushed a 920cc version to the grid as the big Suzuki clearly had a horsepower advantage. They were doing all they could to give their man the best shot.

Dunlop grabbed the race by the scruff and blitzed off into the distance, leading on the first lap by some 11 seconds over the 7.4-mile circuit. There was another factor revealed as the race entered its later stage as Joey, with half a minute lead in the bag, began to ease off. Here Barry Symmons revealed after the race, a bluff card up their sleeve, at least it was a card that surprised Suzuki when Joey did not as anticipated stop to refuel. 'We had put it around before the race that Joey's bike would need to stop. Lap ten was supposed to be the scheduled lap for a rapid top-up but he flew through and it was obvious in the Suzuki pit that the bluff had worked although we didn't really need it.' It was another memorable win for the Ballymoney Bullet.

McElnea's only real chance that day would have been if Joey had had to stop; the Suzuki's did not. And when Joey stormed right through it was obvious that the Championship was decided. Mick Grant was placed

Joey pictured with his long-time friend and mentor David Wood.

Getting your knee down meant just that... no trendy kneesliders for Joey as he pushes the big Honda to the limit.

second with a demoralised McElnea (81) in third spot and Honda team mate Marshall on the 850 in fourth. However, in the 500 race, Marshall put his hammer down to win from Brian Reid with Joey third in front of Con Law.

So Joey became World Champion for the second time and then went back to his favourite pastime of 'sorting' the opposition on his own territory. Mondello Park saw Dunlop rampant with the 'home built' Honda taking him to wins in the FI, Unlimited and the Carroll's Race of the Year. Then came Aghadowey with a 1000cc Race win and first leg victory in the two-part John Player race, but Johnny Rea proved to be equal to his challenge in the second as he kept his 500 Suzuki in front. End of season meetings at Aghadowey and Kirkistown proved if needs be that there was plenty of home grown talent as Joey scored wins, but had to fight hard with the likes of Johnny Rea, Alan Irwin, Courtney Junk and Mark Farmer, who all took places from him.

But he was FI World Champion for the second year on the roads as Freddie Spencer made the 'track racing' World Championship his own. As a postscript to the season, Honda sent a three-man team to Macau; Ron Haslam, Roger Marshall and Yer Maun; Ron and Roger were on the 500s and Joey the FI bike. It was Ron's turn to be rampant, winning in the legs as Roger and Joey swapped second and third places. The Suzuka Eight Hours, as described in Roger Marshall's book, *Roger and Out*, provides an anecdote: 'a deal had been set up by Barry Symmons for two Honda Britain riders to ride a bike for Mr Honda Junior, who had his own bike shop and was obviously very influential.'

'He was desperate to win the prestigious event and Joey and Roger agreed to ride as long as an RVF could be guaranteed and the deal was agreed. The two riders went to see the bike as soon as they arrived on the scene; the bike was named the Little White Bull and was to be an eye opener. It turned out to be a somewhat elderly in-line four. Not unnaturally, both riders were somewhat sick at the thought of the bike's potential performance in an ultimately competitive race. Sure enough the bike was about eight seconds a lap down on the fast men and in any case it expired early on in the race.'

Marshall v Dunlop

team rivalry

1985

Flying Dunlop! Ballacrye and Joey leaps the big Honda. He went on to win with team mate Roger Marshall in second place.

1984 was the year when Honda decided to let Joey and team mate Roger Marshall 'do their own thing,' wrote Jimmy Walker in the *Grand Prix Telegraph* of August 8th, 1990. It was also the year when Joey took the FI Championship for the third time and it really was after a season-long battle with his team mate; and sometimes a battle was reported to be less than friendly. But before that, Aghadowey's opener saw Joey with two wins but a rising Mark Farmer on a 750 Yamaha, put it across his 500 Honda in the 1000 Race. It's worth noting that Robert Dunlop is shown in the results in sixth place in the Ace of Aghadowey Race in which Joey beat Alan Irwin, and that Mark Farmer's 750 Yamaha was Joey's 1980 TT-winner.

It has to be said that while some of Joey's short circuit results in the UK were little better than previous years, he really did make his mark in places where he had not previously shone. A win at Oulton Park on the 500 Honda was notable, and a double at Scarborough was certainly a highlight. Even the Transnationals provided a win at Brands on the 850 in the FI Race and third in the 1300 event, albeit a lowly tenth in the MCN Masters Race in which Wayne Gardner put it across Rob Mac and Roger. Thirds and fourths at Thruxton and Cadwell were also hardly bad, yet Joey was still not getting to grips with the technically demanding features of Donington. He was placed ninth in the World of Sport Race, even if it was just behind notables like Barry Sheene, Ron Haslam, Wayne Gardner and Roger Marshall who had led the procession.

Joey opted for the 750 four-stroke in the 1985 TT whilst team mate Roger Marshall chose the three cylinder, 500cc grand prix two-stroke. Again Joey got it right, beating Roger by 14 seconds.

After that, it was Roger who took second behind Wayne at Snetterton in April with Joey running third. At Oulton Park in May, Wayne again took top honours but this time Joey grabbed second from Roger. Joey was certainly riding as hard as he might as he took an almighty tumble on the 500 and was very lucky to escape with only cuts and bruises.

However, come the North West 200 and Joey was really 'on the pipe' and in a class of his own on local Irish roads, ahead of Steve Parrish and Graham Wood on Yamahas. And so it was back to the Isle of Man, and Joey's by now traditional stamping ground, for a head-to-head with Roger Marshall. It would be the first time that the Formula I Race would be run under the FIM's new 750cc limit.

For the first two laps it looked like a no contest as he took some 24 seconds each lap out of Roger. However, Joey made a somewhat lethargic pit stop on the third and lost most of that lead to let Roger within just four seconds and the race was really on. Joey then went straight back on the pace for the fourth and retrieved a 20 second lead but Roger responded with a fifth lap that was 20 seconds faster than Joey's. Clearly Joey then got the message from his signallers because he went on to break the lap record and set the new time at 19m 32s, a speed just short of 116mph. The win was his by 20 seconds and it had been vintage Dunlop.

Joey shares the elation of victory in this TT paddock shot, with left Steve Cull and Eddie Roberts.

After that win, the best and the worst were yet to come. The best was a new outright lap record in the Senior (500) Race for the course on the fifth lap, at 118.47mph and that left Rob McElnea and Roger trailing. But! That fifth was his last lap and he never completed the race. Looking back on that event, Joey said: 'In the 1984 Senior, I had one hell of a battle with Rob McElnea. We were both on 500s and I stopped on the last lap at the Bungalow when I ran out of petrol. I was concentrating so hard on the race that I came in to refuel on the wrong lap and got totally confused.'

The Junior Race was no better as Joey had Graeme McGregor to contend with on George Beale's 250 EMC and he was flying. They were just 0.2 apart and vying for the first lap lead, but then it all started to slip away from Joey as the edge went off the motor that then cried enough on the fifth.

For the final race of the week, Joey used the big 920 vee-four and had Rob on a 998 Suzuki, and Mick Grant on a 500 two-stroke to contend with. Roger only completed one lap that year as did I. From the start, Joey put in a lap at 19m 34.4s to take the lead with Mick five seconds down and Rob another five behind him. The battle waged fast and furious, and places were juggled on the second when Mac put in two laps at 19.24 to take the lead while Joey had to make the first of his two stops for fuel. Meanwhile, Mick then recorded the fastest second lap time before pitting with Joey. He never really got back into contention as Rob made the most of his one stop

compared to Joey's two, to 'escape' from Dunlop's immediate pursuit and run home with a 14 second advantage at the flag; shades of that famous race in reverse.

So Joey's defence of his FI crown had started well, if perhaps not unexpectedly with a win and he set off for the next round at Holland - Assen. It was Roger's turn to put it across Joey this time however, and in fact he set pole in practice. Nevertheless, it was Joey who got the drop and indeed led right from the start until the time for refuelling. Roger and Joey pitted practically together. This is how Roger saw the incident that started something of a rivalry between the team mates: 'I had a really controversial pit stop. Dunlop said I didn't stop my engine as the rules state you must do when refuelling, but I'm sure that I did. I remember pressing the kill button. Anyway I bounced her off and was out before Joey. I got my head down and pulled away from Dunlop to win the race,' is how Roger reported the incident in his book, *Roger and Out.*

But that wasn't the end of the incident. As Joey saw it, Roger hadn't stopped his motor, and had therefore contravened the rules allowing him to get out into the lead and win the race. He wasn't happy and wanted to

Joey wrestles the big Honda through Rencullen during the 1985 TT.

protest but Symmons, conscious of any resulting bad publicity from team in-fighting, blocked it. However, Mile Pajic took Joey's view and did file an official protest, thrown out by the FIM. The seeds of bad odour were sown.

So they went into the next round in Portugal - Vila Real, level pegging. Portugal wasn't quite as successful as Joey might have hoped. The cut and thrust lasted again until pit stop time after which Marshall gradually pulled clear. But Joey wasn't feeling so good and had to be lifted from the Honda at the finish and stretchered away, quite exhausted. So now it was advantage Roger in the race for the FI title.

For the next FI race, Silverstone's non-championship round at the British Grand Prix, GP competitor Wayne Gardner came to the line as well and proving that competing in the 'Prix' experience was good for his riding skills, he took the win with Roger second and Joey third, ahead of McElnea.

The '84 Ulster GP was critical for the Championship. Roger led by just three points and there was only the round in Belgium to come. I can do no better than repeat Jimmy Walker's account of the final part of that race: 'Joey got home first after an epic race with his ears filled by earth-shattering applause as he beat Marshall in a day to remember. But even after the line had been crossed the drama didn't end, for Marshall shook his fist at Dunlop and he complained that Dunlop had pushed him out at the Windmill in a manner that was dangerous.' Joey's reaction was to say: 'Roger doesn't like being beaten'.

But Roger saw it this way, with half a lap to go and leading as he went into The Windmill. 'I went into the Windmill the quickest that I have ever done, and I just could not believe it when Joey came underneath me, taking a bit of the bank with him in the process. We touched, I had to really run wide, clipping the bank on the other side of the road and then I had to change down two gears to get going again up the climb to Wheelers. All the time Joey was pulling away from me and he eventually took the flag two seconds in front. I was so upset, that I told Barry Symmons that he was a lunatic and I wanted to protest'.

So on to Zolder for the final round. They had shaken hands before the race so as to start with a clean sheet between them. The front row after qualifying consisted of Joey, Roger, Mick Grant and

Eyeing up the opposition, perhaps! No one was cooler on the start line.

Off comes the Arai and no doubt Joey is anxious to discuss how things went with a Honda official.

Roger Burnett on Steve Wynn's Ducati. Dunlop led initially as they all sparred. Marshall squeezed by before retiring with a blown head gasket. Mile Pajic now came through on a Kawasaki as Joey relaxed, knowing that he only had to finish to win the Championship and second was quite good enough; Burnett was third. The World FI Championship was Joey's once again and it was getting to be a habit.

To round off a busy year he returned to home ground for the Killalane meeting and a double in the 250 and 1000. At Mondello Park, the 500 Honda took Joey to the top of the list in the Leinster 200 but he could only manage third to Eddie Roberts and Mark Farmer in the 1000cc Race. It's worth recording that at the September Aghadowey meeting, Joey was placed second three times; Steve Cull grabbed the 1000cc event, Johnny Rea won the John Player Race and it was Cull again who took the Player second leg. And, just for something different, Joey and experienced privateer endurance racer Jim Wells, made the long flight to Japan for the Suzuka Eight Hour Race where they were to retire after 165 laps when lying in sixth position at the time 'the horses' went on strike.

A delighted Joey holds the Jimmy Simpson Trophy for the fastest lap in 1985 around the TT course.

1985 was a very good year for Joey; he even shone on some of the UK short circuits. But best of all was the conclusive manner in which he clinched another FI World Championship, and with a good spread of venues. The story that really made the news in '85 was not simply that of winning the FI yet again, but in the manner that he nearly didn't make the TT, or for that matter, any other race ever again. It was also the year when he gained public recognition for himself and the sport, with the announcement of a Royal award.

Transporting bikes from Ireland to the Isle of Man via a fishing boat was nothing new for Irish racers at the time. What was, was the fact that this trip was almost a total disaster. They had loaded the bikes onto the MV Tornamone and set sail just in time to catch the tide that was on the turn - strongly, on the way out. There are a multitude of rocks in the entrance to Strangford Lough, most of which are adequately covered at high tide. However, just as they left, a missing team member arrived on the quay and got a message relayed to the boat, so the Skipper promptly turned back to effect a hurried pickup; OK thus far.

Sharing in the post race celebrations with Joey are Steve Parrish, left and Tony Rutter, an eight-times TT winner.

Having picked the man up they set off again but by then the water level over the rocks had dropped and the boat crunched onto Irish granite, smashing a large hole in the bottom. The boat quickly began to fill and meanwhile Joey and the others were down below firing up the stove to cook a meal. The accounts following the incident vary, but one has it that the captain decided to abandon ship immediately, and this was the scene that greeted Joey and the rest as they rushed up on deck into the darkness where it was apparent that the vessel was sinking quickly. It was then that another small part of Joey's character came to the fore as he didn't hesitate to take charge of the situation.

Joey recollected: 'Water started to come in and we went to look for the life-jackets and there were none. The captain, he was running about shouting, "every man for himself." He'd a big suit on and he was all right. Some of the men couldn't swim so I started to empty some of the (fuel) jerry cans out in the sea and that started a bit of a row as they said it might start a fire if there was a spark. But I was using the cans for them to float on. We were in the water and I remembered seeing a dinghy lashed to the deck so I swam down and tried to cut it loose. Robert thought it was a bit of a crack but I soon convinced him otherwise. We had to strip all the bikes afterwards to get the water out and I was glad that mine had gone direct from Honda UK.'

So if that was a bad enough start to TT'85 then surely things could only get better - for once they did as the Isle of Man this year was perhaps one of his greatest performances. He was dominant as he wrote his name into the record books with wins in the Junior, FI and Senior, a performance that harked back to the heydays of Hailwood and the TT golden era of the 60s.

Joey started the defence of his FI title once more with a convincing win in the FI Race when Mick Grant on the Suzuki and team mate Roger Marshall both retired, though it should be said that neither had any real answer to his blistering first lap. He set new lap record from a standing start, leaving the record at 116.42mph. That year sticks in my own mind not only for being passed by Joey in the race, but also from dicing on the roads with Nick Jefferies, he on a Yamaha 500 two-stroke four against my quicker, stock GSX-R 750 Suzuki. The same bike, borrowed from Suzuki for a *Motorcycle Sport* road, test proved to be that much quicker than Joey's Honda 400, three cylinder two-stroke in the Production Race. He was, I suspect, somewhat disinterested as he finished in 22nd place, one behind his 'biographer.'

Barry Symmons, long-time Honda team manager, discusses final details with Joey on the start line.

The Junior win was not without incident though. Joey had taken the lead from Brian Reid on the first lap and held it until he pitted on lap three; after that a leak from the filler cap allowed fuel to spray onto his visor in the second half of the race. Meanwhile, Brian made a late charge, breaking the lap record in the process, as Joey's vision became increasingly impaired from the petrol on his visor. However, Brian went out on lap five as Joey won by 15 seconds from Steve Cull.

In Friday's Senior, it was Roger Marshall on the boil and really pushing hard, so hard indeed that he set the fastest lap of the race during the second half. This was on the last lap and he had been closing, riding the 500 Honda two-stroke triple, pitted against Joey's 750 four-stroke. That, however, was too late, as Joey had the race won in the opening two laps, when he took half a minute out of Roger, enough to give him his third win of the week by 14 seconds.

After the TT it was back to Assen for the second round of the FI to win from Mick Grant and Mark Salle on Suzukis. Honda hadn't a bike available for Roger for the series. The following month it was Portugal once more, and with another win under his belt, from Graeme McGregor this time, Dunlop was beginning to look as though he was making the FI World Championship his own and confirmed that with the top spot in Barcelona.

There's a story told by several Joey fans about that trip that came to light afterwards. Joey was driving in Spain, Hubert Gibson was with him. They were on the 'wrong' side of the road and a policeman stopped them for speeding 'a little' over the local limit. The lawman leaned in through the window and harangued what he obviously assumed to be the driver and then proceeded to give an on-the-spot fine of some £70 to Hubert. Joey was seated in what would have been the passenger's seat, that is if the van hadn't been a right hand drive! He studiously looked straight ahead and kept silent as the interchange of pleasantries took place. There were several jars taken on the strength of that little incident.

Joey also had a superb Irish campaign in '85, so much so that it was the occasions that he didn't win that became noteworthy, with talents like Mark Farmer, Woolsey Coulter, Alan Irwin, and Steve Cull collecting the odd scalp from a Dunlop at the peak of his powers.

The year ended on a particularly high note for Joey in that it brought a wider recognition of his abilities. Motor Cycle News readers in their annual poll for Sportsman of the Year, gave their votes to Joey for winning yet again the Formula I World Championship. Honda's Bob McMillan recalls the presentation night as he and Joey waited in a nearby bar for Joey's turn to come up on the stage. Bob well knew that Joey would be nervous on the public platform and had taken him for a couple of drinks beforehand to give his confidence a boost.

Bob carries on: 'We were having a drink prior to the award being made. MCN's man kept coming in as the voting role was announced requesting Joe's attendance. We kept having just one more, eventually they came in again and insisted and we got into the hall as they had counted down to number four. Joe arrived by then in a relaxed and happy state of mind to receive the award and he was really gratified that British fans had voted for him.'

Bob's final word on Joey: 'The man is unique among all of the riders I have known. Once a year I fly over to Northern Ireland to discuss contracts for the coming year. It's usually a fairly convivial meeting and once we agree terms we just shake hands on it and that's it.'

When the New Year's Honours were announced at the end of 1985, Joey Dunlop was listed as awarded the MBE, a fitting end to a year when he clinched his fourth World Championship.

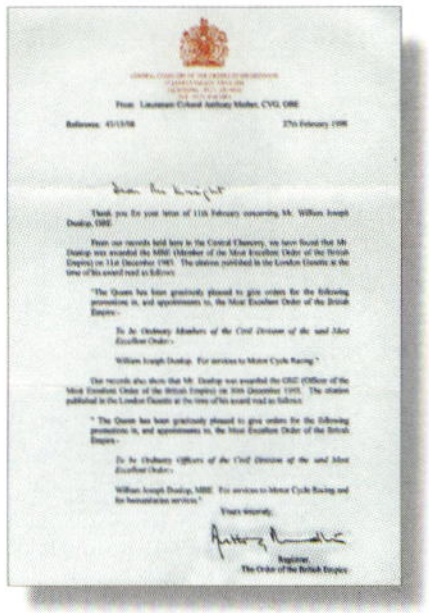

The Honda Race Team Manager during those early years was Barry Symmons and he recalled memories of Joey for this book. 'The proudest moment of my racing career was to see Joey and the family drive away from Power Road to go to The Palace to receive his MBE; and in the Daimler Limousine that I arranged for him through my brother-in-law who had a local hire business. It was always a huge moment of pride for me when Joey won on our bikes'.

'Joey is a man at peace with himself; a man who doesn't suffer fools. A man who sets his own standards and judges his performance by them regardless of other people's expectations. But then Joey is always under terrible pressure from the "Ballymoney Mafia" that always have the highest expectations of him.'

'After a while working with Joey, you learnt to interpret the feedback he would give to the mechanic when coming in after practice. If he said the bike was not so bad, you knew that it was probably terrible. If he said it was terrible, it was probably pretty good.'

'Joey is the most modest of men.'

One of the many pinnacles in the life of Joey Dunlop, a trip to Buckingham Palace to receive his MBE.

3
7
8

The last title

and the MBE

1986-1987

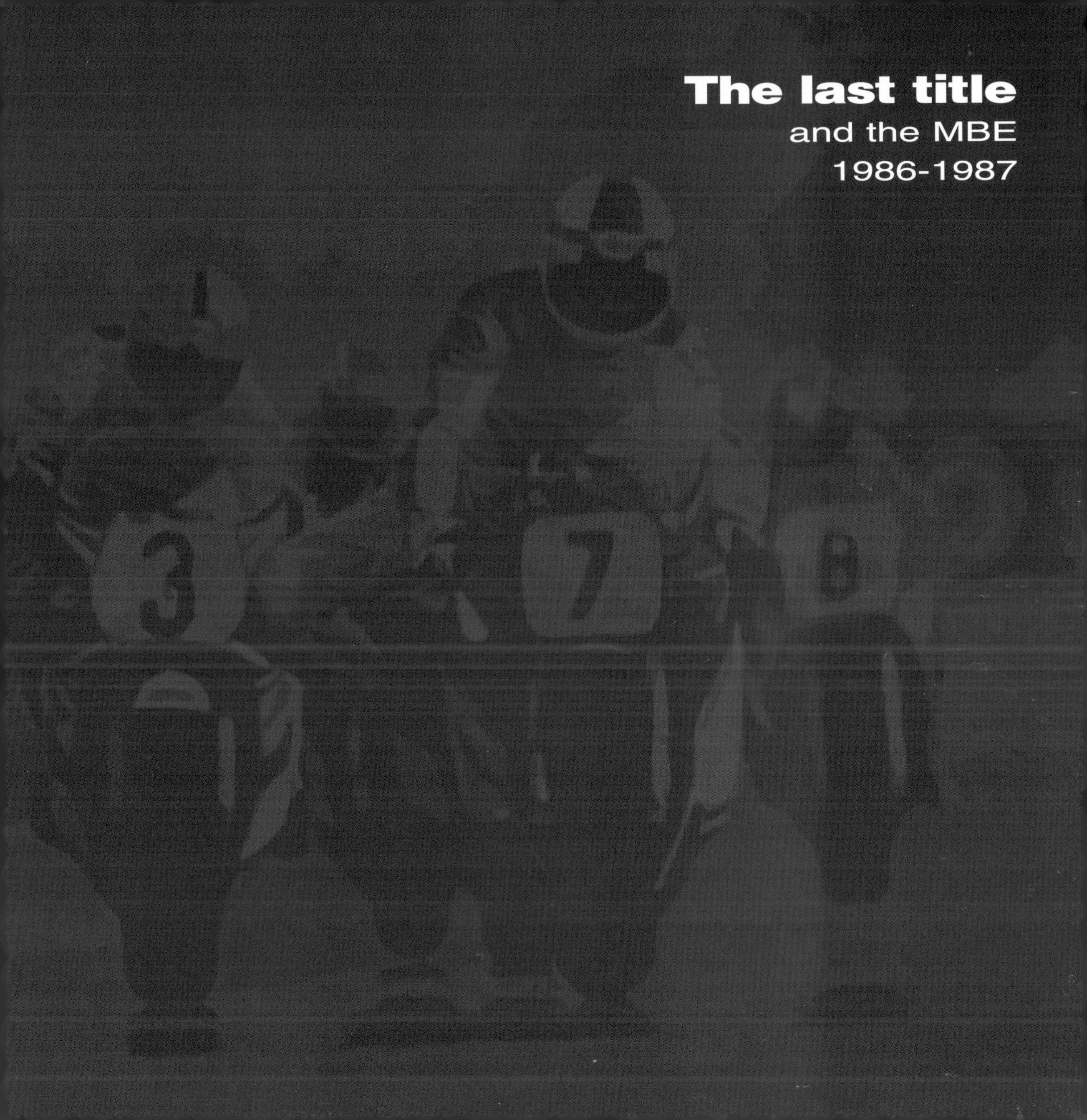

1986 was the year of Joey's first visit to The Palace to receive the MBE from His Royal Highness Prince Charles. It was also the year when he would win a fifth Championship, but Joey was still intent on polishing his short circuit edge and opened the season by venturing over to Cadwell, Brands and Oulton where the going was as tough as usual. At Cadwell, Roger Marshall's protégé, Roger Burnett, beat his mentor for the win in the 1300 British Championship Race while Joey languished in sixth. The Brands result was no better with the same placing but this time Joey was riding his 250. Oulton's British Championship Round was in two legs and Nial McKenzie, having a good season on the 350 Armstrong, won the first with Joey fifth, though things did get better in the second half as Joe, on his 500 Honda, chased Selby's winning Suzuki across the line.

One for the album! A Honda public relations shot at the time Joey received his MBE.

Back on home territory, the North West 200 race provided by now an almost expected win for Joey. There was something of an initial hectic three-way scrap between Dunlop, Marshall and Steve Cull, and that was indeed the finishing order; Joey was riding the 750 Honda, Roger the 500 and Steve the Suzuki 500.

The TT this year came in for some criticism from traditionalists due to, in their view, there being too many production races - four in fact. There were: Classes A,B, C and D, one of which would get Joey his best 'TT Proddie' place. And the weather wasn't being much help either, resulting in Saturday's scheduled FI race being postponed to the Monday and shortened to four laps. But those four laps were the short route to yet another FI Championship round win for Joey. This one was from Geoff Johnson on another Honda. In top form, Joey was never headed and made the fastest lap of the race on lap four, just short of 114mph.

Joey had been entered in the Production Class B race but decided not to take his place on the grid in his least favourite event as the week was beginning to look somewhat fraught with the race being run on the Tuesday due to bad weather. In Wednesday's Junior, Joey's 250 never seemed to be quite on the pace from the start as Brian Reid, Steve Cull and Phil Mellor raced away in front. Joey only made half distance and it seemed he had committed a rare error when he tipped off at Sulby Bridge but it proved accidental rather than a pilot error. It was due to a petrol filler cap that

Joey demonstrates the style that made him so quick around the Island's roads. The Ballacraine Hotel provides the backcloth to this fabulous shot.

leaked after the pit stop, allowing fuel to dribble onto the rear tyre. Fortunately, Sulby Bridge is relatively slow and with no damage to himself, he remounted but a damaged exhaust meant retirement at the pits.

Before Friday's Senior Race, the combined Production Class A and C event took place; 1100s and 600s. The latter would provide Joey with his best Production Class placing on the 400 Honda he rode, in fourth, and earn him another Silver replica; my 18th place on an 1100 Suzuki did not. As a matter of interest our publisher, Malcolm Wheeler, came home two places ahead of Joey in Class C. However, the final race of the week produced a surprising winner, but initially it was Roger Marshall and Trevor Nation battling on time at the front. Nation was on a high from his Production 1100 Suzuki win that morning and he clocked a lap at 19.42.8 on the 500 - Roger was actually 0.8 faster. The other Roger - Burnett, on a Rothman's Honda 500, had tagged onto his team mate's tail and was learning a few wrinkles from his 'instructor' with a time of 19.52.4 - Joey was just over a second quicker than Burnett and was riding his 750.

It looked like Nation's day as he set the fastest race lap on his second circuit and pulled away from Marshall who would be slowed by a chain that had stretched like 'old knicker elastic' and would start to skip over the sprocket. Joey too was having trouble, with his steering damper, and he would spend time in the pits that would deny him another win. Nation's Suzy was reported to have run out of fuel on the fourth lap as Burnett went on for an unexpected win. Geoff Johnson came in second tailed by Barry Woodland as Joey came home in fourth place after being in the pits something like three minutes. It was a TT that did not quite measure up to his usual high standards but in The Island, Lady Luck is a vital team member and she was obviously not on the staff that year.

Production machines were never his favourite mount; this early VFR 750 was no exception.

The '86 Formula I World Championship had opened in April with the round at Misano in Italy and new competition had entered the lists this year; Marco (Lucky) Lucchinelli, on a 750 Ducati. It was he who took the win, but a somewhat eventful one and in any case he would only contest one other round; the Dutch, to finish seventh. In the first instance his Ducati was not so hard on tyres as the fours and he gambled on going straight through but would lose a silencer, and power, en-route. Joey took on fresh rubber at half distance and was 27 seconds behind as a consequence while Marco's rear boot was starting to go off. Joey caught him in the closing stages and was sitting on his pillion, confident of passing the ailing Duke on the last lap. 'But just as I was about to make my move, the bike spluttered and cut out. I tried everything to squeeze a bit of juice into the carbs but she was completely empty,' recalled Dunlop in *Motocourse* of that year. No points.

The Hockenheim round in Germany came next and the 'MBE man' was in command as he made the fastest lap, though Paul Iddon on the works Suzuki chased hard. It was something of a notable ride for Joey as he was caught unaware on the line, adjusting his knee-sliders when the flag went down. He left the start boxed in the middle of the pack and it looked as though he'd a mountain to climb. He and the RVF Honda were quite equal to the task that day though and he rocketed through the field to snatch the lead on lap three. A fuel stop let Iddon on the Suzy to the front but not for long as, lapping some two seconds faster, Joey was in quite devastating form and it wasn't on a road circuit either. He led Paul over the line by eight seconds.

Following his win in the Isle of Man, Joey went to Holland as series leader but he was both lucky and very unlucky this time. Sure he ran out the winner, but Neil Robinson had looked likely to grab the top spot until his drive chain jumped the sprocket and jammed the wheel; a certain Kevin Schwantz beat Iddon out of second place. Now with a clear lead in the Championship, the Honda Team felt they deserved to celebrate and were indulging in a lap of the course much later that day but failed to 'keep the black bits on the road' and overturned the car. Joey finished up under most of the seven bodies packed into the car and broke several ribs among other injuries and although the Spanish round at Jerez was a month later, Joey was not really a fit man come the day. In fact he arrived there with his five broken ribs hardly healed and quite painful when he exerted himself. To compound the problem, the heat was quite stifling and over 100 degrees. It didn't seem to make much difference to Paul Iddon though as he took top honours in front of Graeme McGregor's Ducati, Neil Robinson made third, Anders Andersson fourth while Joey suffering as his ribs bounced on the tank and breathing with difficulty, finished fifth.

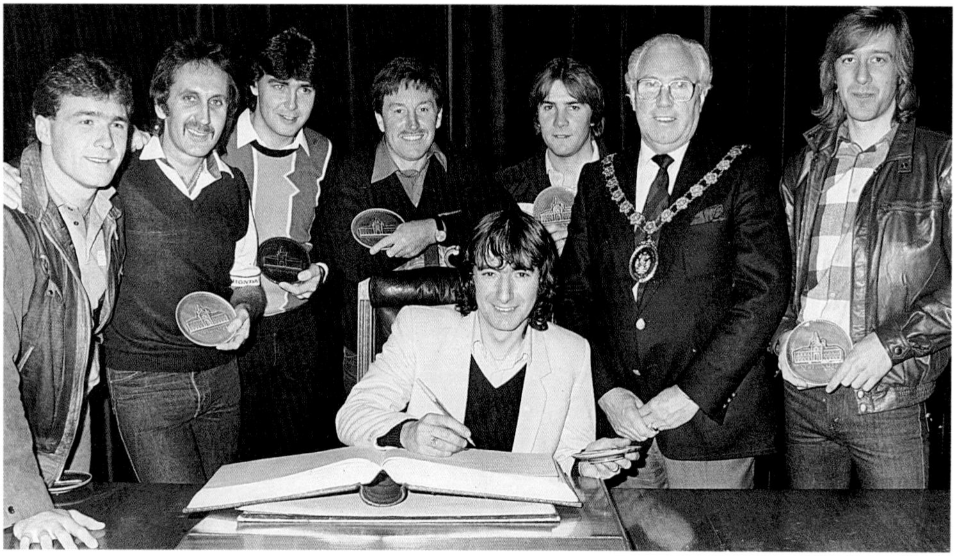

Enjoying the hospitality of the Lord Mayor of Newtownards, Co. Down, Northern Ireland are left to right; Rob McElnea, works Suzuki; Roger Marshall, Rothmans Honda; Roger Burnett, Rothmans Honda; Mick Grant, works Suzuki; Neil Robinson, Keith Heuwen top British privateer and sitting, Joey Dunlop.

Portugal was good. The injuries had healed and the adrenaline was fully flowing. Iddon rode his socks off and was leading Dunlop as the race went into the last couple of laps. He was obviously giving it his best shot as Joey cut a second and a half from each of his last two laps to take the win - by just three seconds. Yer Maun now led the Championship table by 17 points and was looking on course to take the title yet again.

The Imatra street circuit in Finland had something of an infamous reputation from incidents in previous years. The start of the race was the scene of much barging and banging of fairings among the leading bunch and four bikes went down, but Dunlop skirted the melee and, in any case, had only to consolidate his points lead with just the Ulster round to follow. Neil Robinson on the works Suzuki had other ideas however, and was riding a blinder out in front. Joey confessed later to having lost track of the race, but Neil suffered a puncture and Joey missed him, slowing as Iddon came through to second and the unfortunate Robinson limped home a deflated third.

Ireland's big race of the year, the Ulster Grand Prix, was something of a revelation as Joey not only came second in the FI Championship race but he was beaten by a really determined Neil Robinson, set on making amends for his disappointment in the previous round. Joey would later remark 'that he was going so well,' as he just ran away with the race, though Joey's tyre choice was said to be less than ideal. Nevertheless, with second place, Joey won his fifth Championship by 22 points. However, the Classic Senior race would see Joey and Roger Marshall battling hard once more, but with a course record lap at over 120mph, Dunlop took the win. Joey was obviously riding on top form but even so, and just to prove how hard they ride at the Ulster, the 250 race saw Joey in fourth, beaten by Steve Cull, Ian Newton and Mark Farmer.

At the end of the 1986 season, Honda announced that they were to disband their UK race team and instead, direct their support to individual riders through the trade. The fact that competition to Formula I was emerging and would eventually be overtaken by a series based on American Superbike regulations, plus the Superstock Series, obviously influenced their decision, but it would mean that Joey would not have the all-conquering RVF endurance-based bike available for next year's campaign.

There were, of course, many Irish wins, doubles, even trebles, during the year when Joey was not engaged in Championship duties. But the season would finish, like others, with a visit to Japan for the Suzuka meeting in September. They run a class for International Formula Three, which is for machines up to 400cc and very popular in Japan as a stepping stone to higher honours; Joey won that one from Yoichi Yamamoto. There was also a Formula I Race that Honda would not win as Satoshi Tsujimoto took first place on a Suzuki with two other local circuit specialists next and Joey in fourth spot.

1987 and Joey didn't win the FI title. There was a Superbike style Honda for Joey to replace the superb RVF; Bimota-Yamaha would provide very keen competition and Suzuki would be on top form. And in Ireland, Joey would continue his reign.

If the crystal ball suggested that the future of the FI as a World Championship was limited, then this year belied the fact with Bimota entering the fray and the presence of American Fred Merkel would be significant, indeed, it might well have cost Joey a sixth championship win.

This year's North West featured both a Production race and a Superbike race in the programme as well as the usual main events. Joey opened his score with a fourth in the 250 - 350 event, a race won by Gary Cowan, almost dead heating with Brian Reid as Steve Cull and Dunlop were just fractions behind. Joey's win in the proddy race was a pretty straightforward affair on a VFR, which designation clearly signified its origins in Honda's megabuck endurance machine.

New bike the VFR may have been, but the full race-kitted version was pretty good from the start. It conveyed Dunlop to the front of the pack in the '200,' as Irwin, brother Robert, Phil Mellor on what became to be called 'The Beast' (an 1100 Suzuki mounted in a FI chassis) and Eddie Laycock, followed him home in the Superbike Race. Then for good measure he wheeled out the 500 to beat Irwin again and Mellor ran third.

Misano in Italy was now the established opener in the FI championship. The superb Bimota chassis powered by the Yamaha engine looked to be the business, and ridden by Virginio Ferrari and David Tardozzi, would start favourite. But from the off, it was the usual Suzuki duo of Marshall and Iddon who made the running as both Bimotas were sidelined; Ferrari crashed and Tardozzi retired with fuel pump problems. It wasn't Marshall's day either as he also went out; an oil leak due to a gearbox oil seal that didn't. This promoted Joey to a very handy second for a while, that was until Fred Merkel caught Dunlop and snatched the place.

It was off behind the iron curtain to the Hungaroring for the second round where Joey experienced a rare, for him, crash in practice on the new track surface. The two Suzukis again led the field but they too crashed out. However, this left the two Bimotas out in front but not before Tardozzi had

indulged in a barging match, first with Andy McGladdery and then Yer Maun, who survived the experience to finish a somewhat unhappy eighth. This left Peter Rubbato leading on points score with two fourths and 16 points; Ferrari and Iddon on 15 then Joey with 13. But with the Isle of Man round to follow, Joey's challenge looked strong.

While Joey would suffer in practice from a wayward front end on the new bike over the Mountain circuit's bumps and jumps, it really didn't seem to be much of an impediment come the race. On his most favourite of circuits, he scored his fifth consecutive win virtually unchallenged, though Phil Mellor on a Suzuki ran hard in second all the way through and not too far behind to stop Joey getting bored. Rubatto could do no better than seventh and would leave the Island second in the Championship to Joey, just eight points behind.

A little more of the man comes to light in an occasion which Joey and all the family took time out of a very intensive TT race programme, to attend the wedding of TT enthusiasts Gunter Obst and his fiancée Elizabeth. As guests of honour, they delighted the crowd at the wedding in Peel.

The Junior TT Race was perhaps significant, not for the fact that Joey could only manage eighth place in a cracking race won by Eddie Laycock in variable weather, but that a certain Carl Fogarty finished ahead of him in fourth. Fogarty would later figure far more prominently in Joey's career. The 750 Production Race was one that Joey would probably choose not to remember for an eighteenth place, though after the North West performance, it had to be disappointing. 'Mona' was at her weather wise worst come Friday's scheduled Senior; it was atrocious, and the race was postponed to Saturday. This started little better and in the event was only run to four laps and after more delays. The unpredictable weather made tyre choice something of a lottery; some riders thought it shouldn't have been run anyway.

Finally, we all got away and there were torrents of rain in places and when I heard that Joey had wanted to pull out when he came in to refuel, I didn't feel quite so bad after retiring myself after just one lap. The rear wheel on my 1100 Suzuki would spin in a straight line and aquaplane over huge puddles; it was no place for someone racing for the fun of it, and at my time of life, too! While Joey clearly wanted out, he was persuaded to carry on, surviving a challenge from Mellor who would crash, and ran home a clear winner. A mute witness to the atrocious conditions was Dunlop's race average speed of less than 100mph.

The fourth round of the FI series was in Holland and was where it could be said that Merkel cost Joey Dunlop his sixth world title. From the start of the race, the Bimota pair of Ferrari and Tardozzi diced ahead of the Suzuki pair of Marshall and Iddon as Joey and Fred Merkel collided, both contending that it was the others' fault. Uncharacteristically, Joey was seen gesturing from the 'kitty litter' after the disappearing American. Merkel

Big or small machines, it made no difference. Joey is pictured aboard the Gemini 250 Honda. Despite a face full of petrol from a leaking filler cap, he won the race.

would later retire. Ferrari won the race to leave the meeting leading on 30 points as Joey was now two behind and it was on to what would be an Ulster Grand Prix, with weather just as bad as that of the TT.

This was another race that many held should not have been started. Ferrari had already walked out of Dundrod. Norrie Whyte, writing in the programme for the Donington round, quoted him as describing it as a 'nightmare track' and out of date with the speed of modern machines. The race was started in bad conditions but after a lap came the big accident that caused the meeting to be abandoned. Peter Rubatto and Klaus Klein had changed to full wets just before the off. 'We started without a warm-up lap,' said Rubatto, 'Klaus just hit a very deep puddle passing the Grandstand. I lost my team mate and a very good friend.'

1986 AWARDS

Joey was almost involved in that accident, as he remembered the incident: 'I was very scared the time Klaus was killed because I was right in, tight behind him and I couldn't see anything, not even the road. I put my feet down and closed my eyes. I was in top gear as hard as I could go and when I opened them again I was still on the road.' The meeting was abandoned, so Joey left the Ulster still in second place; but for the circumstances he would surely have been leading once more.

The next round held at Sugo in Japan had little effect on the championship since it was dominated by Japanese factory riders. The nearest contender was Anders Andersson in seventh in the race won by Kevin Magee on a Yamaha in what was really a showcase event for the Jap factories on their home ground. Roger Marshall actually ran in third at one stage but crashed out, Joey finished down in twelfth after Ferrari came off after making contact with Joey's back wheel; Iddon and Tardozzi didn't finish.. While the race did not actually affect the leading scores, it robbed Dunlop of another opportunity to score; the tide was running against him through no fault of his own.

Hockenheim was the scene of the last but one round and a one-two for the Bimotas. Ernst Gschwender chased them home on his Suzuki with Joey turning in a good performance in fourth place. This left the scores: Ferrari on 45, Dunlop and Tardozzi tied on 36. Iddon was on 28. And so to the last round at Donington.

Series leader Ferrari had made no secret of the fact that he hated road circuits and came to Donington a clear favourite. Joey's credentials on the roads are beyond question but Donington was never a happy hunting ground. And in any case, the Bimota was far more like a racing machine than the sit-up-and-beg Hondas. 'To me, the championship is a two part event, one for circuit racers like myself and one for the road racers like Joey Dunlop,' said Ferrari; nevertheless the meeting was to throw up a few surprises.

There was a little background to this event as Iddon's bike had been fitted with smaller carburettors and he would gamble on a nonstop run; the rest would pit as usual. It was however, the Team Suzuki Sweden of Anders Anderson who grabbed the lead and held it for the first eight laps; Dunlop had not made a good start and was working his way through the field. A short circuit or not, Joey was fighting to retain the championship as best he knew how and he got into third place on lap ten, passing Anderson in the process, but Merkel in turn got by him.

As Iddon proceeded on his nonstop passage to the flag, Marshall pitted and Joey slipped into second place as Roger then took up the chase again, but the time in the pit was decisive and he was placed second, three seconds in arrears, having passed Dunlop in the process. Joey was to hold onto his third place but as Ferrari came in seventh he kept his points lead by just three. It was all so near yet so far. Luck had been heavily against Joey that year. Any one of a number of incidents either lost, or without them, could have seen him retain the championship once more. If finishing second that year would seem something like a less than successful season, and the passing of a champion, it could hardly be further from the truth.

After the hurly burly of the FI campaign, the trip to Kyalami in South Africa was something of a winter holiday. It was a production race in which Joey, on a bike that he would never get to grips with, would qualify in 28th place and finish well down the field.

Grand Prix superstar Kevin Schwantz (7) added spice to the 1986 Formula One world championship.

PENTHOUSE
Shell
1ST

Fogarty the new pretender

and the big crash
1988-1989

Joey wanted 'his' championship back. He felt that only bad luck had robbed him of a sixth win in 1987 and with a race-prepared RC30, knew that he'd a good chance. The FI series, though not as widely supported by circuit organisers this year, retained its Championship status and Ferrari would not be in the class; it seemed propitious for FI title number six.

This year would be a busy season for Yer Maun because as well as the usual FI Championship, the new World Superbike Championship would run in parallel. Honda had launched the RC30, virtually a racer-on-the-road, to enable them to contest the Superbike series. The principal difference between the two classes was that special frames were allowed in FI but not in Superbikes. Joey would ride in both series.

Easter's six race series Eurolantic Challenge, held at Brands and Donington, was less than successful for 'our Joey.' He was placed 14th twice and 22nd at Brands on Good Friday. At Donington on Sunday and Monday the scores read 17th and 13th twice. However, back to Donington again for the Superbike race in April where Davide Tardozzi was mounted on the Bimota Yamaha with Marco Lucchinelli fielding a Ducati, now grown to 851cc, and it was those two who finished in front of Joey. He was obviously getting to grips with the new bike as he beat Fred Merkel on another Honda and Roger Marshall on Suzuki in the first race. In the second, Lucchinelli took the win with Merkel second, Roger Burnett (Honda) and Fabrizio Pirovano fourth, ahead of Joey. The overall result placed him in third place, which at Donington was a better performance than hitherto.

That Irish classic, the North West 200, was as competitive as usual and was notable for the close finish between Dunlop and Steve Cull. Just 0.01mph separated them at the finish and Joey remembers this one because Cull fell off at York on the last lap as Joey was running low on petrol having to cruise down the Portrush Road with the motor starting to misfire. Meanwhile, Steve had quickly remounted, closed up on Joey and taking him by surprise, stormed by on his RS500 triple (a former Dunlop bike) which, in any case, had the edge on Joey's impaired machine. While Joey had given it his best shot, it was one North West that he must have expected to win.

A proud Joey is congratulated on winning the 1988 Formula One World Championship. Carl Fogarty was of course destined to become four-times World Superbike Champion.

In the 350 race and all on 250 Hondas, Gary Cowan and Woolsey Coulter sparred with Joey for the lead, and close in line astern took the flag in that order. Curiously perhaps, it was the Production Race that gave Joey his only victory at the meeting. As it transpired, Steve Hislop was riding the newly launched RC30 road bike, like Joey, and led the race before 'binning it' at Church Bend, in fact breaking the bike in half, though only sustaining a broken finger. This allowed Joey in second place at the time through to win with nearest pursuer, Richard Rose, on a Suzuki, taking second rostrum spot.

The TT this year was a little different in that the organisers were trying to squeeze some extra race time into the programme and ran the first race on Friday evening; that would normally have been the last practice session. The race was for proddies Class C (600s) and Joey would feature and finish 11th in a race in which the lap record was broken no less than 73 times. It was the scene of an epic duel between Brian Morrison on a CBR and Roger Hurst on the Team Green Kawasaki; I'd even broken the record myself - only to finish down in 25th place.

Saturday saw yet another production race and Joey was again riding an RC30, indeed, many of the 200 brought into the country seemed to be on the grid. It earned Joey a fifth place in a race won by Steve Hislop. That three lapper was just a warm up for the competitors in the Formula I six laps. I watched pure vintage Dunlop as he blitzed off into the distance to blow away the received wisdom around the paddock that he was up against it this year; only having a race kitted RC30 and not the familiar RVF. Certainly he hadn't shone in practice. Carl Fogarty recorded fourth and Paul Iddon fifth to score themselves valuable points in the Championship. It was in fact scoring fourth that persuaded Foggy to try contesting more FI rounds and would prove to be crucial in deciding the outcome of the Championship that year.

Wednesday's Junior Race combined the usual two strokes, to 350, plus FII 600cc machines - FII was being phased out and the machines were being given a last crack. It was actually Steve Hislop on a Yamaha 350 who made the fastest lap. However, it was on the last lap of the race, by which time Joey had once more run out in front of the field on his 250 Honda, never to be seriously challenged and to record his second win of the week.

Joey didn't turn out for the Production A Class race on his entered CBR1000F and it has to be said that as far as TT racing is concerned, was a bit of a tank. Joey obviously thought better of it and saved his energies for the big one on Friday; the Senior TT. This race was a corker with Steve Cull on top form and always looking as though he might sneak the win, but Joey left the line to open his charge with a new lap record from a standing start at over 118mph, while Cull was just four seconds behind. But then Steve cracked in a new lap record at 119mph, to snatch the lead on lap two; split seconds separated them and Hislop was also in hot pursuit.

Cull's challenge was to fade in the later stages and I well remember seeing his bike on fire, parked against the bank on the run down to Brandish; the fire was due to an electrical short. It was quite off-putting at the time, on the approach with head on the tank and doing all of 145mph, I'd thought it was a crash. So Joey scored yet one more win as Hislop turned the wick up a shade higher to consolidate his second place.

The Formula I Championship series then went on to Holland once more where Joey had something of a troubled race, finishing a lowly eighth. Carl Fogarty could do no better than ninth as Roger Burnett was on top form on the day to take the win. Joey finished fourth in the next race in Portugal, which was not contested by Burnett as it coincided with a Superbike round. Rain fell heavily on the event in Vila Real and would cause the race to be stopped and restarted. Fogarty had performed something of a rain dance in the first half and was in the lead when it was stopped. He did likewise in the second but nevertheless, water would be the cause of his 'exit' as it found a way into the electrics.

In Finland, at Kouvola, Joey finished third. Carl was once more just a place behind but still racking up the points. But for Joey, the Ulster that year was a disaster where the Championship started to go awry. The weather again played a vital part in the result. Dunlop started the race on slicks as it looked as though the track would dry out. Luck being what it is at times, it never did and he had to stop and change over to intermediates giving him no chance of getting anywhere near the front; he finished down in seventh as Foggy won from Steve Hislop. That points haul left Carl just 5.5 points behind Joey and suddenly he looked like a champion in waiting.

In 1988 he clinched the Senior Trophy. Pictured on the rostrum with him is Steve Hislop, third and Geoff Johnson, second.

In Pergusa, on the streets of Sicily, the race was a total disaster in that it never really happened. Joey didn't make the grid and now for the first time, Carl took the lead on points as he grabbed the win from Gianluca Galasso on a works Bimota. Joey related how he believes that he lost his FI title that year by giving Fogarty bits from his bike. During practice he fell going into the chicane; a momentary navigation error when 'just riding along' waiting for Fogarty. A consequence of that crash was that his tyres were allocated to Carl.

While it was only a comparatively low speed tumble, Joey was quite badly shaken, and indeed injured, and finished up in the local hospital overnight. Though they let him out of hospital early in the morning, as long time recorder of Joey's career, Ivor Davidson, recalled the incident: 'Joey had badly bruised his shoulder but in any case had qualified in fifth place in the final morning's session. Immediately before the race the bike just would not start and it seemed like a broken valve spring. 'However, Joey thought it was likely that the motor had taken in sand in the crash.

Now there was just Donington to come and if Joey could finish on the leaderboard, the title could still be his again but the real problem was that Fogarty had only to get into the top ten. It didn't look good and in the event it certainly wasn't. Fogarty was initially some way ahead of Joey and informed via pit signals was content to hold his position. When it became obvious that it was in the bag he later speeded up to slot into fifth place and win the FI title. Joey finished a disappointing 11th place after a day that he would want to forget and the title had again eluded him; yet taking the season into account there could so easily have been a different result.

The year of the big crash - 1989

A triple TT win in 1988 was just about as high a highlight as could be, but nevertheless that season hadn't been a good one for Joey. It was beginning to look as though the tide was turning against the man who had become to be known by more than his Irish fans as the King of the Roads, as well as the King of the Mountain and The People's Champion. But if 1988 was a bad year, then 1989 would be the worst of all in his already long and illustrious career.

Joey chose to make one more trip to the UK and Brands Hatch in particular, for the Easter weekend meetings. But this one was fateful. The pack had hammered into Paddock Bend jostling fairings as usual, but Belgian Stephane Mertens, riding on the inside of Dunlop, lost it and slid underneath Joey, scooping him up and causing his crash into the banking and tangled up with the bike. 'The Maun' was well bent and he was taken to the nearby St. Mary's Hospital at Sidcup. Like my own visit to that establishment, it was not a happy one, if any visit to a hospital for injury could be.

I suppose it has to be acknowledged that motorcycle causalities are somewhat frequent in a hospital adjacent to Brands Hatch and that they probably regard motorcycle racing causalities as self inflicted injuries at a time when they already have enough to do. My own experience could not compare to a man with broken thigh, leg, wrist and several ribs as well as multiple bumps, bruises and abrasions.

Joey's stay was some ten days, after which experience he was told that he would never race again. Far from home and friends and so dejected, he was ready to discharge himself and go home in the back of a mate's Ford Transit on a mattress. Dunlop was at his lowest ebb.

He suffered two operations on his leg. After the first, a second job was necessary. Then he was told that there wasn't very much more they could do to repair the damage to his wrist, that according to the specialist, would never be the same again. Enter Honda's Bob McMillan, who was being kept informed of how his Irish hero was doing and took the bull by the horns and had Joey flown home to be taken care of in Ireland. The Irish specialist took a more encouraging view and operated again and for months afterwards, Joey had to soak the wrist in hot water every morning to get it moving and have hospital manipulation to try and restore full movement. It was the first of many countless hours of exercises on the long road back to health.

Once the wrist could function Joey was able to get back on a bike but he had an 18 inch pin down the inside of his leg which started to move about. Scheduled to stay in place for nine months the pin began to protrude from the hip so it was back on the operating table to remove it, something the doctors were reluctant to do at the time. The bones were healing sure enough once Joey had all the bits in the right places, but like all such injuries it is the muscles that take the most trouble to get back to full working order, and eventually, strength. Within months he was itching to get back into

Remembering the man. A picture that paints a thousand words about motorcycle racing at the highest level. A fly-spattered helmet and a fairing almost devoid of colour. It is a poignant reminder of a man who brought so much to pure road racing both at home and overseas.

the saddle but it was asking rather too much for Joey to ride his usual bikes. David Wood came up with a solution by starting a team within a team; persuading Andy McMenemy to provide a 125 Honda for Joey to make his comeback on. Even with muscles still somewhat wasted, it was just possible for him to manage the small, light bike.

Joey Dunlop actually got back onto the tarmac competitively at Fore road races on Sunday 16th July. Good Friday seemed a world away but a gritty Dunlop grimly piloted Andy's machine to the finish in eighth place. The general view at the time seemed to be that Joey would never be the same man again. Some felt that he should rest on his considerable honours and long years of success that any other man would settle for; but not Joey.

A week later at the Munster 100 in Co. Cork, Joey again mixed it with the other lightweight contestants in the up to 200cc class. Even after a week, improvement was noticeable. This time Joey was fifth but more significantly, whereas last week he'd been some seven miles per hour on average slower than winner Alan Caughey, this week it was just a three mph deficit. Three more weeks gave time for more exercise and healing and it was brother Robert who won the class at the Mid-Antrim by a street but this time Joey made the last place on the rostrum behind Michael Topping and the old spark could be discerned still burning. He did ride the 250 but this was still asking too much in a race won by Johnny Rea.

There were other meetings, even trying the 750 in places, but it was the Ulster GP that was a milestone in the comeback story. Joey rode in the FI Race. Hislop just beat Fogarty for the win chased by Steve Cull on the Rotary Norton; Joey rode to a lowly 20th place and was lapped. He finished exhausted and in considerable pain from half way through the race and said that he had only kept going for his thousands of supporters. Twelve months later he would win there again to confound his critics who had been quick to write him off. And the McMenemy 125 would provide him with famous victories in later years that he might not have had but for that big crash at Brands.

As a footnote to the end of that year, Bob McMillan has a particular memory of the TT where Joey was still not fit enough to ride. The organiser's were keen for the current Mountain Course hero to be part of the TT Festival. He was in the programme, the entries having been made before the crash; Joey had even entertained the idea of riding to the point of arriving at the meeting with a medical certificate from his own doctor that certified him fit to race, but it was not to be. The ACU stewards took one look at Dunlop, now a shadow of his former self and limping badly and ordered him to be examined by their own doctors.

The convened medical panel took the view that Joey just did not have enough strength in his right arm to control a bike over the humps and bumps of the course. However, the organisers did manage to get Yer Maun onto the circuit for the benefit and acclaim of his thousands of fans. Bob gave Joey a ride around the course in between races on the back of a CBR1000. 'We kept slowing down to ride slowly past crowds of cheering fans, and then speeding up to catch up with the travelling marshal who was escorting us round.' After the ride Joey said, 'I'm not getting on the back of that bloody motorbike ever again.'

'I'll remember one particular incident on that ride that will always stick in my mind,' continued Bob. 'There was this old couple walking slowly down the pavement at the side of the road listening to a portable radio as the announcer was recording Joey's progress round the course. They wanted to reach a gate where they were to give the man a cheer as we rode by. It was typical of the sympathetic support that Joey got from the waving crowds that year.' As Bob told me later, quoting a remark by Phillip McCallen: 'When Joey decides he's got his race head on, he's unbeatable round the Isle of Man.' He would be again.

Joey Dunlop
Arai

Fighting back, the long haul

McMenemy and the 125

Joey went back to the familiar Irish meetings to continue his struggle for fitness and the competitive edge that he felt would surely return. Mondello, Kirkistown and Aghadowey saw Joey in unaccustomed places down the field on both the 125 and the 250. However, a flash of the old brilliance flickered at Cookstown when he beat Steve Haslett's EMC to win the 250 race and make the fastest lap. In the North West, further progress could be discerned, not that 13th on the 250 was too much to write home about but it certainly was a top class field. If that wasn't notable, then the fact that he rode the 750 into fourth in the second Superbike race behind brother Robert whizzing the Rotary to top honours in front of Phillip McCallen and Eddie Laycock - that certainly was progress. Additionally, in placing fourth on the 125, his speed was genuinely competitive.

The TT FI Race had now been downgraded by the FIM to 'Cup' status as Superbikes came to the fore on the International scene. Circuit owners preferred to stage events that they saw as more popular; not that Joey would contest either so early on in his battle back to the top.

Being anything less than 100 per cent fit for a TT race is quite enough of a handicap for any rider. It was a race in which Foggy and Hislop rode RVF's that Honda had brought in, it was said, in order to make sure that Yamaha, celebrating their 30th year, would not to be able to celebrate with a victory. Foggy's bike would go to Joey for the Senior race as Fogarty would attend to Superbike duties in the USA. The two hotshots were trading fastest laps at over 120mph throughout practice and their rivalry was obvious.

In the FI event, Joey rode his RC30 to a steady eighth as Foggy took the win, chased home by Nick Jefferies on a Yamaha and brother Robert on the Norton. After a troubled start to the race, Steve had made the fastest lap at 122.63mph, eventually finishing right behind Joey. However, the honours were not entirely missing that year as Joey made up the Manufacturer's winning team with Foggy and Hizzie.

The 125 only carried Joey for a couple of laps but Robert was starting his run of wins. In the Junior, the 250 lasted just three of the four laps and it clearly was not a good year. While Joey hadn't been too far off the pace on the smaller bikes, he did make the full race distance to 16th place in the Senior, though he was never in the hunt. The Isle of Man demands total commitment just to compete, to win demands a rider at his best. His fans could be heard saying, 'Wait 'till next year.'

The fight back to full fitness continued in Ireland as Joey could now run regularly at the front and a win came at Skerries Milverton circuit on the 125, plus a couple of thirds on the 250 and third on the 750. In public, the man was now quite clearly regaining his form; in private the exercises continued as muscles were painfully hammered back into shape. A win on the 250 at the Temple, with a fastest lap, was a prelude to the Ulster and a real milestone that said the man was back.

Rain masters. With little thought for the weather, Steve Hislop tracks Joey during the 1990 TT.

A brotherly rivalry was already developing when Joey and Robert rode the little bikes and the 125 race at the Ulster was quite something. Sure Robert won but the margin was a hairsbreadth; Robert averaged 104.77mph; Joe 104.75mph and they made joint fastest lap at 106.118mph. While Brian Reid captured the top spot in the Junior Prince of the Roads event on his 250 Yamaha, Joey spent the race jousting with Steve Hislop being just 0.4mph behind at the flag and both lapping at 116.8mph. But the big one was a race that Joey well remembers, having fitted the standard carbs to improve fuel consumption and to attempt a non-stop run; echoes of his famous TT win.

Right from the start of the race, Joey shadowed Robert, slipstreaming his faster rotary Norton and 'short shifting' wherever he could, doing a passable imitation of an economy run. Sure enough, as Robert and then the

Like a jockey over the sticks, Joey found the perfect balance to handle all kinds of machinery. He was particularly at home on the 125s.

Honda Team pitted to take on fuel, he sped on to take the victory raising his hand in salute as he crossed the line. That small demonstration of Joey's delight at the finish of that race - the uncharacteristic waved fist in the air as he saluted the flag - said it all. It really had been such a long route back, a testimony to the steel hidden within the quiet man. The celebrations continued for some while afterwards.

To Joey Dunlop it had been a long fight back to the top after all those races riding round in the middle of the pack. A lesser man would have called

To the delight of huge crowds, a nail-biting finish saw Steve Hislop pip Joey to the line in the 1991 Senior.

it a day and many couldn't have stomached finishing behind men who wouldn't have seen which way he went before the crash. There are many instances in the Dunlop annals where it can be seen that when Joey really sets his mind on something, the man is totally focused and will succeed for himself.

Back on top in '91

Aghadowey had always been a happy hunting ground for Joey and the first meeting of the year on March 16th saw Dunlop score a win and second place on the McMenemy 125. For good measure this was followed by a second and fourth on the 250 and there could be no doubt that he still possessed the competitive drive to seek out competition wherever it was offered. Indeed, he followed that up with a first time visit to Nuts Corner's short scratchy circuit; went on to Mondello Park and if they did not see Joey 'first under the linen', then Aghadowey once more, was something of a landmark as he beat Phillip McCallen on the 750 and chased home Robert on the 125.

Phillip was something of the 'new kid on the block' by now and the man to beat but Joey was the man pushing him, twice at Kirkistown, also swapping places with Johnny Rea. If Joey's performances were not yet quite as all-conquering as in the years before the big crash; come the Tandragee meeting it was only Phillip again and Robert who could keep in front of him. The 250 race recorded McCallen's race speed at 98.83mph and a mere fraction behind was Joe on 98.82mph in a close and exciting

Brothers they may have been but when the flag dropped it was every man for himself. Here they are pictured at the Ulster Grand Prix, not one of them prepared to give a quarter. Robert aboard the John Player Norton pushes the machinery to the limit while Joey looks up the track, no doubt planning his next move.

On this occasion at the Ulster, it was brother Robert that Joey had to overhaul. Quick on the gas, the rotary Norton pushes out the familiar blue smoke as Joey sets off in hot pursuit on the RC30.

tussle. Kirkistown continued the return to form as Joey trumped Phillip in the 750 race and won the Norman Brown Memorial race on his 250 ahead of Jeremy McWilliams and that man McCallen.

Joey has scored some notable performances at the North West 200 through the years although he professes not to class it as one of his favourites, being hard on engines and cycle parts and not always having had the best of luck. Nevertheless, Norton were having a good run that year with the Rotary and Trevor Nation was on a high as he won the second Superbike race, but with them both clocking laps at over 121mph it was Joey who was making the challenge to finish just 0.2s behind. Robert won the 125 from Joey and in the 250-350 race, Ian Lougher, Robert, Brian Reid and Yer Maun himself, were running nose to tail, averaging 113mph, and could all have been covered by the proverbial blanket at the finish in that order. It was a pretty good '200' all things considered.

Joey said that he still hadn't quite the full strength needed to fight the bike around the TT's 37.7 miles of jumps and bumps but nevertheless he was still capable of a practice lap at over 120mph. But with Hislop and Fogarty putting laps in at 124mph and 123 mph on the mighty RVF's, it did look as though Joey was 'Team B.' Just for something different, he was fielding John Harris's CBR Honda in the 600 race and had put in a practice lap at 110mph, in spite of not liking 'treads,' or indeed any production bikes.

On a perfect day for racing, Saturday's TT Formula I event was a battle between the virtually unchallenged high speed duo; one that Dunlop was not to join, completing just one lap before retiring to the pits. In the combined 125 and 400 event, the talk in the paddock was of the chances of Joey beating brother Robert and equalling Mike Hailwood's record of 14 TT wins. However, Robert had cracked his own lap record in practice by 30 seconds with a lap at over 106mph, whereas Joey was on 101mph and only in 6th place on the leader board. It looked as though Joey had a mountain to climb, but then he never did set much store by really fast practice laps, usually having several bikes to set up and in any case often deliberately not choosing to reveal his form.

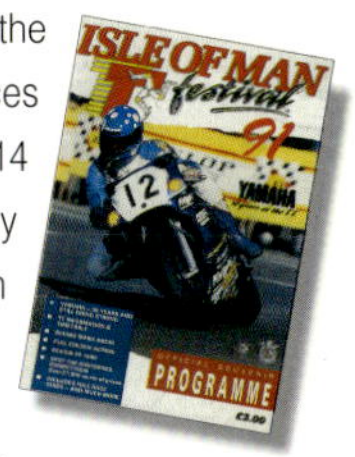

Joey looked as though he might be doing a disappearing act on the first lap of that race as he was 22 seconds faster than Robert. While Robert pulled back a couple of seconds on the next, it was in the pits at the half-way stage of the four-lap race where it all went wrong. The night before, Joey had decided to fit a quick-filler petrol cap with breather pipe rather than a 'quick screw' one with breather pipe. The pipe had started to work loose during the first two laps; then the filler cap had been hard to close. Petrol had gushed out of the breather and all-in-all, it was a pit stop that went wrong when it should have saved the odd vital second in a race where they would all count. That protracted refuelling blew the race for Joey as he lost over half a minute and by the end of lap three, Robert was leading by 17 seconds. There would be no 14th win this day as Joey settled for second and Robert cracked in a new lap record on the last at over 106mph.

Though Joey was a member of the winning club team with Robert and Johnny Rea for the MCRRC of Ireland, he had what he would describe as a steady ride in the 250 race, finishing in fifth as Robert put it across Phillip. Riding the Harris Honda later in the day, Joey recorded a lap at 114mph on the last lap to slot into sixth, beginning to get to grips with the 'strange feel'

of treaded tyres, as opposed to racing slicks. This was good enough for yet another Manufacturer's team prize along with fellow members Hislop, who won, and McCallen in fifth.

The Senior race was billed as having its 80th anniversary with Joey inheriting Foggy's RVF for this race, while Carl was away on Superbike duties. The result never seemed in doubt as Steve Hislop dominated the race all the way through. But then Joey's second place was never really in jeopardy either, in spite of Trevor Nation's challenge on the first lap and Brian Morrison lapping at over 121mph on the second, just a couple of seconds behind Joey. Phillip made a late charge to finish third for a Honda one-two-three and wrapped up the Manufacturer's prize yet again.

If Joey reckoned that he wasn't quite 100 per cent fit for the Mountain course that year, then he certainly was for the Billown circuit when he returned to the Isle of Man for the Southern 100. He just blitzed the meeting with five straight wins from the two 250 and three unlimited races plus a first 125 in the combined class event up to 600. If the field did not contain too many 'names,' Ian Lougher and Steve Hazlett kept their 250 Yamahas in hot pursuit, though on the 750, Dave Leach never looked like improving on second place.

Joey and Phillip McCallen continued something of a season long personal duel in the big classes and Robert did likewise on the 125. At the Ulster, Robert seemed to have the advantage and indeed was winning the class more often than not; but Joey was only 0.2 behind at the flag in something of a furious chase in which Robert made the fastest lap by just one mile per hour. It was vintage Dunlop in both Superbike races with two wins by the narrowest of margins; Phillip made the fastest lap in both events, being denied the victories by fractions of a second on the line.

The 250 class often provided a three-way scrap and as at Fore, for instance, Robert could be seen at the head of the field to beat both Phillip and his elder brother. Joey certainly scored some real highlights in '91, but the downside of that were the occasions when he clearly was not going to win. At Skerries, Phillip was dominant on 250 and 750, though Joey snatched the 125 from Robert. At Carrowdore, Joey had to settle for just a 125 win over Dennis McCullough, but seventh in the 250 and third on the big one as Leach followed McCallen home.

Using the telegraph pole as a sight, Joey launches the John Harris 600 Honda across Balaugh Bridge.

The season rounded off with the Sunflower International at Kirkistown but this attracted some heavyweight opposition. It was Carl Fogarty beating Rob McElnea by a fraction in the Senior race, followed by Brian Morrison, Simon Crafar, Eddie Laycock, Alan Irwin and McCallen as Joey chased them home. Robert scooped the 125 from Davy Lemon as Joey followed on in third.

For so long Ballymoney's most famous citizen, Joey Dunlop received civic recognition of the fact when he was made Freeman of the Borough in 1992, only the second person to receive that honour, and a fitting accolade.

If 1991 was not a particularly memorable year, though high spots there certainly were, then '92 would be a year when he would start an incredible five year run of TT wins. He would equal the late and great Mike-the-Bike's long-standing 14 TT wins record, though wins 'at home' would be sparse.

Brother Robert's growing domination of the 125cc class and his three TT wins was something that was beginning to niggle Joey; he'd had the 125 TT race win in sight last year only to have it slip from his grasp in the pits. Brothers they might be, but competitors they certainly were, and would give no quarter when there was a race win in prospect. Joey decided that the 125 TT this year would be one that he would win - at least he'd give himself every possible competitive advantage.

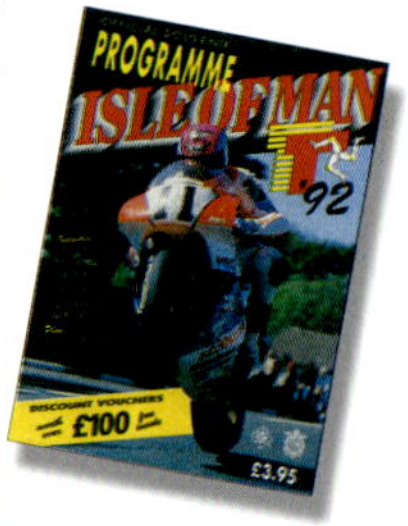

He adopted an unprecedented regime of dieting some weeks before the TT as power-to-weight is everything on a 125 but he still did not look to be anything like the top man after practice. In fact all the front runners in the class put in their fastest times in the last day of practice as the weather finally came good. Robert topped the list on Friday evening with a time of 21.42.8 at 104.26mph, some six seconds in front of Denis McCullough who'd made his time in the early morning session, but Joey languished down in eighth, over half a minute behind his younger brother.

If he seemed to be off the pace in the small class then he'd hardly looked like it on the mighty RC45, recording a practice lap at just short of 120mph for fourth place overall. Third in the FI race could hardly be a bad result either, though it did look as though Honda just for once might not

On his way to yet another TT victory, 125 Honda mounted, in a class the Dunlop brothers made their own.

actually win the race as Foggy held the lead on his Yamaha for four laps before gearbox cogs cried enough at The Bungalow. Phillip had pursued furiously but had also been chased hard by Steve Hislop on the overheating 'rotating Norton;' Joey had run behind the trio and finished up in one more Manufacturers Team Award with Nick Jefferies making the third. As a footnote to this race, the tank mountings on the 750 had broken in the race and he'd had to resort to holding the tank in position with his knees; something of déja-vu from 1977 on the Rea Yamaha.

The mid-day sun casts a shadow over a master at work on the Island roads.

With the grid comprised almost entirely of Hondas (Francesca Giodano fielded an Aprilia), the 125 race was one for the record books blowing way out of sight all previous figures as Joey and Robert fought for every split second. Robert rode number 54 in the split race grid as the 400s went away first; Joey followed on number 59 - 50 seconds behind on time. The faster 125s would soon get amongst the slower 400s; they both passed me!

They both cracked in standing start lap at over 105mph but it was Joey who was just 3.6 seconds faster with the pace getting even hotter on lap two. This time Robert went quickest; both were over 107mph and as they were reported as dead heating around the course; Robert pulled back all but 0.2 of Joey's lead and that was the time difference between them. Unlike last year, Joey's pit stop gave him the advantage this year and he was 7.4s in the lead at the end of the third lap. The last lap was an absolute cracker with less than a second separating the brothers on time and both lapping over 108mph.

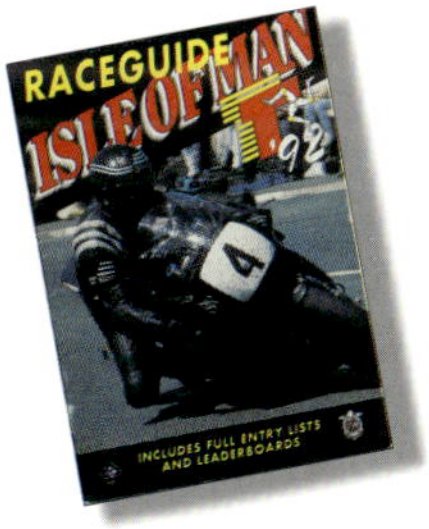

Joey finally scored his 14th TT victory, equalling Mike Hailwood's record by just 9.4 seconds from Robert and it was obvious that it gave him a lot of satisfaction. There had been so much discussion of the possibility that Joey remembers: 'A lot of people were glad that I did beat it and got it over with. It used to annoy me. It got to the stage when I was afraid at times, because there were that many people talking about not wanting it beaten. I was afraid that something would happen so that I wouldn't beat it. It annoyed me a lot at the time.'

Wednesday's Junior race saw Yer Maun retire in the pits with a broken gear change lever after just two laps running fourth/fifth. In the afternoon,

Joey came to the line on the Harris Honda in the Supersport 600 event, though this race would be somewhat problematic. Michelin had fitted new boots to the wheels the day before and it appears that pressures were not checked before the race. After another slide, Joey was aware by Laurel Bank that things were not all they might be. He nevertheless soldiered on and finished ninth. Back in the paddock, when asked what sort of a ride he'd had, Joey grinned and pointed to the rear tyre. It was shredded almost down to the canvas. There was just 18lbs pressure in it. However, ninth was still good enough for the Team prize with Phillip and Steve; 13 places in front of yours truly.

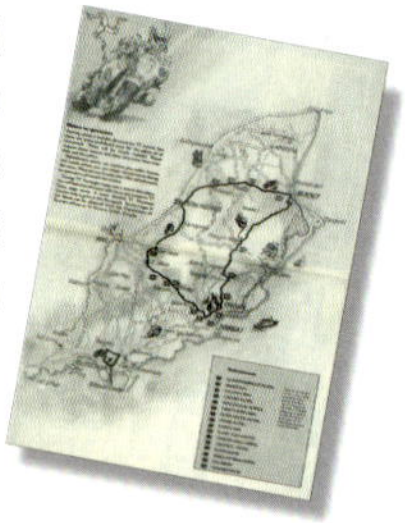

The Senior race really was one that Honda didn't win this time and memorable it was too, with new figures for the record books for race and lap, as a British bike won the Blue Riband event of the week. Steve Hislop on the 'White Charger' Norton put across the Loctite Yamaha ridden by Carl Fogarty after trading laps all the way through. Robert got the second Norton into third as Joey got no further than the pits on the second lap.

The Irish season hadn't been an auspicious one for Joey Dunlop but a departure for him was to compete in some Classic races on a Seeley with no results that I could find. A win on the McMenemy Honda in the Ulster just in front of Mick Lofthouse was one to savour, while, at the Isle of Man Steam Packet Races after the TT, beating Denis McCullough in an almost dead heat race and defeating Phillip on the 750, was certainly memorable. But when you have a record like the man from Ballymoney, anything less than top placing tends to pale, though there is a long list of them.

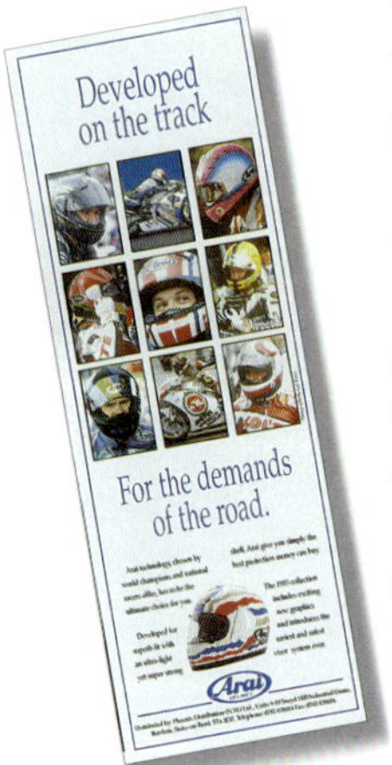

Neil Tuxworth, Honda Race Team Manager, on Joey

'I grew up with Joey in a manner of speaking. I raced with him in the early 70s and then I started to work with him when I joined Honda at the end of '89.

Joey is a rider that will do his own thing. You can only control him to a certain degree. We were not going to change him. He is very set in his ways. Promotion and publicity aren't the big thing with Joey although he understands the need for them.

I have tremendous respect for him. I keep saying to people when they rule him out, that you never can rule Joey Dunlop out when he is riding in the TT, and is always capable of winning one more.

Somebody asked me the other day about Phillip taking over as the main man at the TT but to me Phillip is a very good TT rider while Joey is a great TT rider. And in my opinion there's a big difference.

Joey is very much like Hailwood in many ways. He judges a race exactly and rides the course superbly, always on line and dead smooth. Phillip on the other hand is totally different and aggressive. He'll sometimes

Dunlop on Michelin! Joey adopts a gentle approach to Ballacraine.

take a different line on every lap and look out of control. As Steve Hislop and I were saying, unless he changes his style he'll never go any faster. He'll never go any faster than he is now because he isn't tidy enough. So that's the difference between Phillip and Joey. Both are nice guys but entirely different personalities.

I've the greatest respect for him on and off the track. And the things he does for charity are absolutely amazing. Joey is very good at organising himself. Off the track he is very much the family man. He just likes to get away from things and do his own thing.

He's not one to be in the limelight, he'd rather drink with his mates in the pub. That's just Joey basically. There will never be another Joey Dunlop. He's an absolute legend.'

YAMAHA

Fifteenth TT win

and the Irish 600 Champion

1993-1994

Robert Dunlop savours the moment after winning the 1991, 125 TT. He pushed Joey in to second spot, Bob Heath third.

Revitalised would best describe Joey's Irish performances this year, something that seems to be repeated throughout the later chapters of this book. He opted for a full campaign in Ireland contesting the Regal 600 Series on the Harris CBR and won it and left records in the books that still stand (at the time of writing). In the TT - as well as winning the 125, there really had been a chance of snatching a Senior race from Phillip.

Joey opened his victory score in '93 at the first Aghadowey meeting on his 250, in the second race; Paul Harrison had beaten him in the first. No real scores at Aghadowey's second meeting or at Kirkstown but at Cookstown the Dunlop bandwagon resumed its old momentum. The 1000 Race was a win from Derek Young but in the 250, 'hot youngster' James Courtney, just managed to fend off Joey on the 250, but not before he'd made the fastest lap.

Tandragee was good too as Joey again won the big race from Young and put it across Brian Reid and James in winning the 250 event. However, brother Robert grabbed the 125 as James harassed Joey but couldn't quite make it stick by the narrowest of margins - just 0.02s. The North West this year would not be as good as usual for Joey, as younger brother Robert won both 125 and 250 races and Carl Fogarty twice put it across Robert in the Superbike races - both on Ducatis. Joey was third in the first and fifth in the second, hardly bad; indeed in the second, Phillip McCallen and Rob Holden chased the leading pair home with Joey closely in attendance in a pretty keen race.

And, so on to one more TT and after all the Isle of Man Tourist Trophy rides that Joey had had since 1976, the Formula I race was one that Joey described after the race as, 'the worst ever TT ride I've had after something broke in the rear suspension.' He finally finished in 14th place. But it was win number 15 on the 125 as Joey really had the race won on the first lap by taking eight seconds away from Robert who was always lapping a shade slower, though he did take back six seconds on the pit stop lap. They both lapped at record speed on the last circuit as Joey clocked 21m 52.2, a speed of 108.55mph and faster than Robert by five seconds.

The Junior race was simply Brian Reid's day, though Jim Moodie, Robert and Joey had all practically matched lap times. Indeed, Robert made fastest lap by a couple of seconds as he almost displaced Jim in second place with Joey just the odd second in arrears. It wasn't Robert's day though as he retired on the last lap letting Joey onto the rostrum in third.

The Regal Championship regulations require standard bore motors but the TT regulations at the time allowed an overbore by one millimetre - and it made a difference. John Harris had built Joey a 'big' motor for the TT and I'd taken it from Crowborough to the Island for him. Joey said that it had felt strong in practice and times were good in spite of only completing starting and stopping single laps. But the best laid plans etc. After a lap running on the leader board, the second time through The Bungalow and the motor had suddenly 'gone rough and I thought it'd blow if I carried on so I just parked it,' said Joey. The reason was simple. The standard tank's fuel switch has an internal pipe extension that provides road riders with a reserve, usually removed for racing. But, it hadn't been and it wasn't possible to do two laps without this modification, permitting the use of the tank's full capacity. As the fuel runs out, the motor coughs first on one

cylinder and then another. It feels as though it's falling apart for a moment before stopping. At least that's how it had felt on my own Harris CBR one year when some kind soul had switched reserve off before the race and I was set for a Replica and a top 20 spot, too.

Luck was against Dunlop in the Senior race in which, at Glen Helen on the first lap, he and McCallen were dead-heating. Joey was really on the boil, but a hose that ducted air from the fairing vent, through the tank and into the airbox, was working loose, upsetting the fuel injection system and causing a misfire. Pitting on the prescribed second lap, the best that could be done to remedy the problem was simply to try and tape it in place, which resulted in Joey falling some 40 seconds behind Phillip McCallen. The hose would be replaced in the second refuelling stop but the delay would result in an 11th place finish.

Back to Ireland for the Skerries and Robert just won both 125 races from Joey, but he rounded off the day with a win, in the 350 and 1000cc races as if to prove he was still Yer Maun. The four miles-plus road circuit, at Fore in July, was really good for a resurgent Dunlop with four wins and a second out of five; only Robert could take one; the 125. The following Temple 100 provided a 125 win but the Ulster's 125 race was something of a blanket affair, though pocket handkerchief might have been a more accurate description of the battle between Robert, Mick Lofthouse and Joey, in that order at the finish. The 750 race was another cracker, as the Honda trio of McCallen Joey and Nick Jefferies duelled at speeds over 118mph with Robert Holden right behind chasing them home - that blanket description might have fitted this one, too.

Apart from Joey's win in the Regal round at the Mid-Antrim, there were seconds in the smaller classes where Reid and Dunlop the younger did the business by split seconds. The season had been the best since the long fight back through 91/92. And as it drew to a conclusion, there were more wins to add to a score just like the old days; 125 twice from Robert at Dundalk, 600 and 250 at Carrowdore, the 125 at Killalane and lots of other places on the way. It finished with Joey 600cc Irish Champion (the campaign is the subject of chapter 13) and that at least was a new experience to add to his illustrious record score.

It was a clean sweep for Honda in 1994, pictured left to right are Phillip McCallen, Steve Hislop and Joey.

In 1994 the TT wins just kept on coming

The North West 200 was by now old hat for Joey but it was my debut ride at that event. There was a good scrap in the 250/S400 race between Woolsey Coulter, the McCallen man and Joey, but Ian Newton put it across their Hondas on his Aprilia and that's how they finished. In the 600 Supersport race, the new Yamaha outgunned the Hondas. Phillip and Joey's CBR's were not likely to win from Mike Edwards, Ian Simpson and Mark Farmer - the order at the flag. Joey and Phillip were in close company on their RC45 Hondas in the second Superbike race, but just in front of them there was a little drama being played out. Robert scored the win, but it was a fraction in front of Ian Simpson on a Yamaha who had clocked the fastest lap, managing to lead on occasion. However, Ian was disqualified after the race when his motor was measured oversize, placing Joey third, Phillip second and to Dunlop the Younger, the laurels.

As a portent of things to come, Joey displayed his old form at the Tandragee, just before setting off for the Isle of Man. The Young challenger, Courtney, had to give best to the 'old man' on the 125 while Alan Irwin and Ian King had to do likewise in the Senior race. The new RC45 was obviously a winner but when pitted against the Island's undulations, it proved to be something of a wayward beast and required much setting up during practice week. This did not prevent Steve Hislop, on his return to the Honda Team, from easily topping the practice leader board at 123.53mph though reportedly on the ragged edge, and it has to be said that he looked to be the man to beat. Joey was seventh.

The Saturday's Formula I race was a debacle that only Manx weather can inflict upon a race programme. Most of the top runners had started on slicks but by Ramsey it was raining heavily and chaos reigned (rained!) as riders came into the pits for a change of tyres, with some demanding that the race be stopped; Joey like many others called it a day in the pits. It was privateer Nigel Davies on intermediates who led the race on lap two when conditions had just started to improve and the organisers stopped the race.

A look that says so much. Joey shares his success at the TT with his then Manager David Wood. It was a very special relationship that lasted for a large part of Joey's career. To Joey he was more than a Manager, he was a mentor, confidante and above all, a great friend. In the centre is fanatical TT supporter Luke Lawlor.

A race hadn't been run on Sunday since the seamen's strike back in 1966, but the organisers wanted to keep the race programme on schedule during the following week so instead of the usual 'Mad Sunday' melee of road riders over the Mountain it was FI again. Hislop confirmed his Island talent once more by leading from start to finish. McCallen had taken too long to get his act together to mount a challenge but it was a disaster for Robert Dunlop who had the rear wheel on his RC45 collapse while driving out of Ballaugh. He was badly injured. Joey had a race-long tussle with Steve Ward before annexing one more third place and Team Prize.

The 125s this year were sharing the grid with the single cylinder bangers. With Robert out, this race looked like a gift to Joey but he really did have second thoughts about even starting the race. 'I was very nervous, even when I was racing it never left my mind. I was going to pull out because Robert was bad and we didn't know the way things were going to go,' said Joey. In the event, Joey walked his way to his 16th win and dedicated it to his brother who was by then starting to come out of danger. In the afternoon's Supersport 600 race, Joey finished in seventh place in spite of lapping at 115mph. This wasn't far off race winning pace, but in such a closely contested event won by Ian Duffus on a Yamaha, it just wasn't sufficient even to get on the leader board, such is the level of competition in the Supersport 600 class.

The Junior Race provided Joey with win 17, one he didn't realise until he got back into the paddock. It had started badly for him, the brake-side footrest was loose and would spin round. He recalled the incidents leading up to the race. 'We were working late (before the

Always neat and tidy on the slow bits, but it was on the fast sections where Joey really made up the time.

race) that night and I told this chap to remember to go right over the bike in the morning. The footrests were the only thing he didn't check. I had to ride with my leg held in all the time and it got badly cramped.' McCallen had looked to be on a certain win with Joey still struggling in second place, though he did even chip into his lead at one stage. But a pit stop in which Phillip didn't take on quite enough fuel, gifted the race to Joey, who coined the old adage: 'you have to finish to win', as he did so with the footrest hanging off!

'I have no plans to retire from racing,' said the evergreen road racing phenomenon that is Joey Dunlop after his 17th TT victory. Surely the best was over. It certainly wasn't for Joey but it was for me my last and 32nd Mountain racing year. The Senior race produced the same result as Saturday's FI event: Hislop, McCallen, Dunlop.

Before going on to what turned out to be a memorable Ulster, victories came thick and fast: both smaller classes at Dundrod, a clean sweep in all classes at Skerries and 125, 250 and Senior at the Mid-Antrim. It looked as though Joey had turned the clock back a decade and any remaining doubters, if indeed there were any by now, were effectively silenced.

Ulster Grand Prix '94 was memorable, not just for another win, but in the manner of him achieving it. Joey won the 125 narrowly from Ian Lougher and Phillip; the first Junior race from James Courtney with Joey in tow. In the second, it was McCallen again as Joey beat his 'young pretender' (James) this time. But it was the first Superbike race that would be inscribed in the record books of the famous race. Dunlop and McCallen were dicing for the lead. They were side-by-side going down to the Hairpin

A fine example of Joey's style. A perfect line, time after time, was the secret of his success.

but Joey couldn't quite get the RC45 stopped in time. In a detour down the slip road, he rejoined the race seven seconds in arrears.

It was a race to remember, as with the fans urging him on, Joey sliced into McCallen's lead and eventually caught him on the last lap, to Phillip's considerable surprise. Joey was in front going down into Quarries, racing for the flag and Dunlop recalled the incident when McCallen just got too desperate to retake the lead. 'He put a hole in my leathers and it was brave 'n tight. There was no room where he was trying to pass me. I think he got a shock seeing me go by instead of Jason (Griffiths - who had been second after Joey went down the slip road). He only had between the Hairpin and Quarries to get me and I made sure he wasn't going to. He tried the impossible. I think it was the only time I've ever had any bother with Phillip and I've had some really good races with him.'

Joey actually made a somewhat belated Manx Grand Prix debut in '94, riding for Isle of Man enthusiast Terry Teece. The story started at the Southern 100 paddock where Terry approached David Wood to ask whether Joey might consider riding his 250 Aermacchi in the Manx for a bit of fun. To David's response: 'Well ask him yourself, he's there.' ...'Joey, would you like to ride in the Manx on my 'Macchi?' brought forth the simple answer - 'Yes!' As Terry recalled, 'There was no incentive. No money involved, he just did it for the love of the sport. He was fantastic.'

The little Aermacchi didn't last very long though; one lap in fact. As Terry Teece saw it, Joey was just too fast for the bike and was virtually riding it flat against the stop all the way around the course. Joey related to Terry afterwards: 'I went down Bray Hill and saw a flash come out of the carburettor, when it stopped.' When the Bladen brothers, who had fettled the motor, stripped it down for the post mortem, they found the exhaust valve in the carb. This wasn't quite the end of Joey's Manx Grand Prix career however, as Terry promised Joey a competitive 350 for the following year.

So to take the second instalment out of calendar context and recall the 1995 MGP, Terry related that Joey 'used up' several gearboxes. 'He had been used to ignition shifting on modern machinery and, I think that he was using the same technique. But an Aermacchi is not designed to rev at 11,000 and the gearboxes don't respond kindly either. For the race, we fitted a rev limiter, but with hindsight it wasn't really compatible with the ignition system we were using and it overheated and cut the revs down until it would only do 7,800. Third place and a lap at over 98mph just has to be a very good result.

'You'd ask Joey how the bike was when he came off and he would always say, OK,' recalls Terry. 'Though there was one occasion when I asked him how the brakes were and he said something to the effect that he could stop quicker by putting his feet down. Then we happened to notice that the forks had deflected so far under braking that the front tyre had been rubbing on the engine. But I suppose that is the difference between modern twin discs and a classic brake. Then I remember the time when Chris Bladen had rebuilt the gearbox again and had the bike ready for Thursday afternoon practice. When Joey turned up he had obviously been involved in a seriously long celebration the night before, and Chris rather laconically remarked to Joey that he was glad that he was 'taking things really seriously.'

But Terry recalls the man with immense respect. 'He is one of a kind. He just rode for fun and thoroughly enjoyed it. What other rider of his calibre would do that? They just broke the mould after that man.'

Joey's trip to New Zealand in the winter of '94 is one that came out of the MNZ's (*Motorcycling New Zealand*) successful attempt during the TT to take the Maudes trophy back home. They had fielded a team of ten Kiwi riders, including eight complete newcomers to the Mountain circuit, on standard Yamaha 600s who, in all finishing the race at an average speed over 100mph, were awarded the trophy by the ACU for this most meritorious performance.

What resulted from that became something of an Irish Team Tour; there were a few Brits. It came out of ideas sparked between the accompanying officials of MNZ and Billy Nutt, who masterminded the Irish end of the scheme. Joey was to be the lead rider and main attraction. The idea was simply that the team would be able to spend a couple of the UK's winter months honing their riding skills and also taking in a holiday, instead of 'hibernating' in the snows in Northern Ireland.

Joey was accompanied by nine other Irish riders among the 16-strong

Ian Duffus, Ian Simpson, shadowed by Joey in the 1994 Supersport 600 race at the Island.

party of competitors from the UK. Among them were names like Denis McCullough and Ian Lougher; MGP winner Emlyn Hughes and George Burns, as well as a band of 'helpers' all guaranteed to make the most of the many convivial occasions that presented themselves before and after the meetings, held through November and December. It's something of an Irish custom for participants in such celebrations, that any member who falls asleep before the party is over is liable to lose one eyebrow, removed by dilapidary cream, of which more anon!

Stu Newby was among the band of enthusiasts who accompanied the party and among the anecdotes that he calls to mind was when Joey and his band were staying in private accommodation in Auckland, where they were told to make themselves at home. Joey came down to breakfast on the first morning clothed in very little and when asked by one of his team if he was going to put on anything else in front of his hosts responded: 'Well this is how I am when I'm home.'

There are men from the Emerald Isle found all around the world holding key positions and New Zealand has its full share. A local customs officer with Irish antecedents was able to process the agricultural and customs procedures within the hour when the bikes arrived by plane, somewhat behind schedule and during free practice for the Baypark meeting. The assistance was something that Stu attributes as typical of the influence that Joey had upon many of the people involved, often at very short notice, in making the team work smoothly. While they were hanging about, Joey was checking out the circuit and was told by a marshal to 'clear off as this is a restricted area.' Later, learning who the man was, his chagrin was a picture to behold and his mates have not forgotten the incident long afterwards.

Another example given by Stu, was that after the bikes had been cleared Joey had his taken to the house at which his team were staying for race preparation. Being aware that closing time was approaching, Joey asked that a request be made to the manager of the host Irish pub for them to stay open a little longer so that they could have a night-cap. This turned into a two-in-the-morning session at which several eyebrows were forfeited. It's worth recording that Joey was one of few in the team to survive the tour with both eyebrows intact.

A bus journey was arranged to take the visitors from the Tauranga circuit to the next track on the schedule in lower North Island and in the event it took a lot longer than expected, due to the many stops on the way and a few more eyebrows lost. On the tour, a meet-the-riders evening for the team had to be delayed, while the organiser of this evening, after verbally chastising everybody for being late, had to persuade Joey to get off the bus after he had threatened to stay on board and go back to Tauranga. You don't harangue Joey.

After several nights out visiting Irish pubs, Joey was heard to remark that there were more Irish pubs in New Zealand than there were back home. Typical of the man and how he likes his own space and travelling, is that after arriving in South Island, he requested the loan of a van and sleeping bag and took off: 'Just to have a bit of a look round.'

Stu Newby sums up the man by quoting one of the very many people who would turn up at circuits where Joey was racing. 'Just to see the legendary Irishman, who liked a smoke and a drink and who could foot it with the best at the Isle of Man, even though he was forty-plus.'

It has to be said that the tour was more of a holiday than a full race calendar. Equipped with his 125, Joey competed in the NZ F3 Class that included a large variety of bikes that in other countries get a race of their own. In Kiwiland, in order to make up full grids, F3 comprises GP 125s, multi-cylinder four-strokes up to 400, 600cc twins, 250 and open class single bangers, with only two valves and 500cc air-cooled engines. Among few results shown in the record books and given the competition, to finish seventh at Pukekohe was actually a creditable performance.

At Mansfield, things were not quite so good as the 125 was not behaving too well only managing a DNF in the first race and 14th in the second. At Christchurch things looked up as there was a race just for 125 GP bikes and here it really was a proper job with the likes of Ian Lougher on his Aprilia grabbing the win from Denis McCullough and Joey on their RS Hondas.

And so back to the chills of winter to prepare for yet another season.

DUCKHAMS
HONDA
JOHN HARRIS MOTORCYCLES
FERODO

The John Harris connection

1993 saw something new for Joey; winning the 600 Regal and Irish Championships. John Harris had prepared a Honda CBR600, mainly for Joey to ride in the TT, but this year Joey would keep the bike at home and contest the full season. It turned out to be a fiercely contested and memorable year in which he would score notable wins and set new lap records for the class. It stands out not just for those accomplishments, rather for the fact of Joey's self confessed lack of enthusiasm for racing production machines, despite two wins at the North West, but for the fact that he became the man to beat in the class.

To recall how Joey came to be riding the 600 in the first place: in 1991, Honda had launched the CBR-FM, a complete redesign of their 600 that was being overtaken in the performance stakes by the likes of Yamaha and Kawasaki. They wanted to see it on the tracks in the Supersport classes as a highly visible promotion so they supplied selected dealers with machines at a special price as an incentive for them to put Honda 600s on the grid. John Harris, with a business of that name in Crowborough, Sussex, was already dipping his toe into racing by supporting myself on a CBR and took up the challenge of entering a bike in the UK series for the class. As it happened, John's venture didn't work out after the rider crashed and the bike languished in the workshop. But more later.

John takes up the story: 'Having been to every TT since 1968, I was fortunate enough to see Joey in action through the late 70s and 80s and had built up a great admiration for his riding ability. That plus the fact that he seemed to be a thoroughly nice bloke, something borne out when I was introduced to him prior to the TT Supersport Race in 1991.'

'Imagine my initial disbelief and delight when I got a call from Honda Team race Manager Neil Tuxworth, requesting that the machine we were entering on UK short circuits be made available to Joey for the TT. He rode in practice and declared it, "Right enough." Those four laps of the 1991 TT Supersport Race were the longest four laps of any TT that I have ever watched. The sixth place finish was great and Joey said that he enjoyed the race and that was a grand start.'

John and brother Steve were delighted to have a man like Joey on board and this started a four year machine association on that bike, and a long standing friendship. Visits to Northern Ireland became regular to support Joey while he was riding the 600 and John and his wife Sally became regular 'lodgers' with Lee and David Wood, Joey's putative manager at the time.

John continued: 'I had gone over for the Mid-Antrim races in August and while Joey was going well on the bike, the twistgrip kept sticking, to the point where he retired. However, in the evening at, The Railway Tavern, Joey presented me with a glass slipper which was almost life-size. He poured a bottle of Bacardi in it, added a small amount of Coke, mixed it with a wheel nut wrench and handed it to me, so he was of some assistance in the fact of my achieving a state of considerable merriment.'

'After the event, I vaguely remember standing on a table in the small hours and, ably assisted by Joey, reciting *The Green Hills of Antrim are Calling to Me*. I'm sure I never knew the words, still don't, and finished up arm wrestling with Joey. David Wood then spent the rest of what remained of the night sitting up with me; he was so concerned about the amount of alcohol that I had consumed. Later, David related how that he then had some difficulty in getting me back to the airport the next morning. Apparently he kept putting me in one side of his car and I kept getting out the other. He eventually managed to pour me onto the plane just before it took off.'

'Joey is a man with hidden depths, that you just would never suspect. We were together at Mettet and I'd ridden out there on an ST1100 to meet him; he was by himself and I was mechanicing for him on the 125 and 250. With no pressure on him and no public spotlight beaming on his every move, he chatted away all day like a gramophone and you just would not recognise the introverted Honda Team Man expected to deliver results in front of thousands of fans at the TT.'

'A particular instance comes to mind at that meeting when Joey crashed the 250 in practice. The rear end was twisted and this called for a prime example of "Irish engineering" that was to afford the crowd gathering outside the garage some entertainment; it seems they could hardly believe their eyes. There was some building work being carried out at the back of the pits and there was some equipment left there while the meeting was in progress. With the aid of some scaffolding and planks we were able to lever the rear sub-frame back into shape, Joey applying final persuasion with a large building block. That it bolted back into place perfectly just goes to show what is possible and what Joey is capable of.'

Joey had led the race, albeit narrowly, all the way through, but was troubled by a front brake in which the lever was coming right up to the bar and was having to 'pump it up' approaching every corner. It was a component that had been crunched in the fall and the replacement wasn't behaving itself. Right at the last bend and being pushed hard, a momentary lack of brakes took Joey out wide, which created a chance that local champion, Marc Fissette, seized like a dog pouncing on a bone to take the race pushing Joey into second place.

It is worth recording the 1993 season that Joey had on John's 600 on the Irish circuits contesting the Regal 600 Championship. It was a tooth and nail scrap all the way through in every round, with some notable performances against up and coming youngsters and established hard men; men like Ian King, Alan Irwin, Brian Reid, Johnny Rea and James Courtney. The Regal Series had good prize money and attracted the top men on well-prepared machines. The man who was by then old enough to be a father to most of them would roll back the years, as only he could do, to produce performances that any of them would be proud of.

The first round of the Regal Championship took place at Cookstown and would set the pattern for the season to come in producing razor sharp dicing. Joey threw the gauntlet down by setting the fastest lap and leading Alan Irwin across the line, and he was practically neck and neck with Brian Reid with Ian King fourth.

A week later on May 1st at the Tandragee 100, things were even more furious with Johnny Rea joining in the fun. Yer Maun won this one too, but it was Ian King making the fastest lap in finishing second as he and Rea banged fairings, a fraction behind, with Irwin and Reid in close attendance. This level of cut and thrust raised the series to ever-higher popularity

Hang on! Joey puts the CBR suspension to the test over Ballaugh Bridge.

among the enthusiastic crowds and brought back memories of the Armoy Armada v Dromara Destroyers battles to the older enthusiasts.

On to that old favourite the North West 200 meeting and here Joey had more than the home-grown talent to contend with, in the shape of Jim Moodie and Mike Edwards. This was one that Joey didn't win, but it was hardly for the want of trying, setting a lap record that still stands (at the time of writing) at 115.619mph and finishing in third place ahead of Bob Jackson and Brian Reid. However, Moodie and Edwards would not contest the series, so this was as good as a win.

After Joey's somewhat rocket assisted-start to the Regal Championship, things did not quite go according to plan at the Dundrod 150 where Johnny Rea narrowly scooped the win on his Yamaha from Derek Young. In spite of making the second-fastest timed lap, Joey had to settle for fifth in a race as closely contested as usual, but with Ian King in third and Gardiner fourth; the points position had closed up a little.

Derek Young won the Skerries round from King and the scrapping duo had drawn clear of Joey in third place which meant that the series looked to be up for grabs as they were now close on points. Fore's four-mile road circuit, is one that Joey always liked and so clearly did Ian King. The 600 race was the scene of a real humdinger of a battle with King making the 'Master of the Mountain' dig really deep to win, but by no more than a wheel. They were separated on time by just one hundredth of a second.

Another visit to the Isle of Man's Southern 100 meeting, in which he won the 600 class, next saw Joey at the Temple 100 where he again made the fastest lap, but didn't win. Indeed, winner Reid and second placed Young grabbed the one-two in a race in which Joey had looked to be on for another victory after having made most of the running. But he got it wrong on the last corner in a mighty rush for the finish. Third was still good enough to beat King in sixth place by several points.

Derek Young and Ian King continued their season-long Regal battle at the Mid-Antrim but it was behind Yer Maun who took the win, after which Joe headed the now traditional skirmish at Carrowdore. He chalked up another first, with yet another fastest lap, to narrowly put it across Ian who was now looking like the man who might deny him the series win. Come the Killalane meeting and Joey finished fifth. But it was without Ian King who had non-started due to injury at a previous meeting, so Joey drew further ahead on points to wrap up the series and added a new title to his illustrious list; that of Irish and Regal 600 Champion.

John gave a small insight into the character of the man: 'Joey is curiously charismatic. Not in the way that public figures are usually thought to be. It's a lower key sensation. You gradually become aware of his presence. You increasingly develop a respect for the man. He is a man that it takes time to get close to. Joey is a very inward type of person, in the nicest possible way, very quiet and thoughtful and as honest as the day is long.'

'It might be difficult to engage him in a conversation at a meeting and perhaps that is understandable given the pressures on him to deliver. However, an unsuspected side of Joey is that he can be quite witty on occasion. There was the time when we were at a continental meeting where the supplied fuel was somewhat less than ditchwater in octane rating. Joey went out to practice on the 250 but it seized. He spent ages cleaning up the damaged bore where traces of piston metal remained and had put the old piston to one side.'

'Meanwhile, next to us in the paddock was a rider sponsored by a Japanese gentleman and his rider had seized his 125 for the same reason and had it stripped down. As the gentleman viewed the slight 'witness' of metal left by the seizure and exclaimed that it really had seized, Joey moved over and said: 'That's not a seizure,' and with a flourish, proffered the piston with its great scores down the sides and with some emphasis said - This is a seizure.'

The OBE, Europe again

and nineteenth TT win, 1995

This year, a number of European race organisers got together to set up what they called a 'Pure Roads' Series. Ireland's Billy Nutt was one of the prime movers in the series which covered events at Mettet in Belgium, NW 200; Ulster Grand Prix; Riga in Latvia and Tallin in Estonia.

To open his European campaign of '95, Joey ventured over to Mettet, for the first round of the Championship, where he won the 125 and was second on the 250 after an eventful ride, recounted in the last chapter. Next came Tallin, one of those meetings where Joey was watched by a huge crowd who wanted to see Yer Man do his stuff. He brilliantly justified their faith when he took wins in 125, 250 and Superbike races. For good measure there were fastest laps in each.

The TT in 1995 was a great one for Joey and one in which I was able to take a more personal interest than usual as I was no longer riding myself, due to a big 'off.' It was a year not just notable for the fact that he scored a superb TT double, it might even have been a treble, but the fact of Joey simply blowing the opposition away in winning the Senior and 250 races and a real head-to-head in the Formula I race with Phillip McCallen. He was certainly the star of the show and seemed to be defying the 'gravity' that Anno Domini imposes on lesser mortals.

Joey was awarded the OBE in 1995 for his humanitarian work and became the first British motorcycle racer to receive both the MBE and OBE.

Saturday's FI race programme opener was to provide something of an epic duel between the team mates on the RC45s. Phillip McCallen had been a late recruit to the Honda Team, to augment what had been scathingly referred to in the press as the 'Dad's Army' team of Dunlop, Nick Jefferies and Steve Ward. They scored 120 years between them! It looked as though Honda were conscious of the strengthening opposition from Ducati and Kawasaki and wanted to be sure of maintaining their hold on the race they had won so many times that they practically took a proprietorial interest in the result.

From a standing start, Joey and Phillip lapped at over 120mph; there were just three and a half seconds between them. They sparred on time, though not on the roads. Joey was riding his familiar No 3, while Phillip riding No 9 started a minute behind Dunlop. As the lead swung fractionally back and forth between them, both had trouble that the crowds lining the course could not be aware of.

Phillip confessed afterwards to keeping his head up too much on the first two laps and as a consequence was peering through a fly spattered visor. Joey was losing top end power as a hose ducting air from the fairing to the air box was coming loose. Nevertheless, it was Joe who led after lap two; still that three and a half seconds gap. Both took on fresh rear boots but refitting the hose cost him a lot of time in the pits. So Phillip led by 25 seconds at the end of lap three.

Neat and tidy as always at Ballacrye on a V&M Honda in 1995.

Lap four and Joey had reduced that gap to 12 seconds and was

A superb shot of Dunlop blasting through Kirk Michael in 1995.

charging and the interval was down to eight at the end of the fifth. McCallen though was in some trouble as his rear suspension unit was starting to fade and the handling was deteriorating badly. In fact, it was bad enough for Phillip to say after the race that he was considering a stop at the end of the fifth to check the rear end but, realising that it would cost him the win, soldiered on to victory. Joey said that he was happy with second place but clearly he felt that he'd been robbed of another notch in his tally. The race was a real crowd pleaser to open the week of racing.

High noon! Even the greatest suffer from nerves on the start line. Joey makes his way to the start line accompanied by David Wood on the left.

There's something of a story behind Joey's win in the Junior event. The nature of the win had its origins in the abortive (for him) morning's 125 race, which, if anything in racing in The Island is sure, was his best chance of a win. During interview in the paddock before the off Joey said: 'The 125 must be the best chance as I've managed a nearly 109mph lap.' There's nothing truer than you have to finish to win a race. Look at last year's 250 when Phillip McCallen went out when leading.' Those words were to prove prophetic.

The day had dawned dull and a little chilly. Temperature has a marked effect on performance of the little single cylinder two-strokes in the Ultra-Lightweight race and several of the machines had the ubiquitous 'duct' tape over portions of their radiators to ensure that optimum working temperatures were reached: Joe had some on his, too.

While the race itself produced a dramatic last lap with Mark Baldwin snatching the win, the bulletin read: 'No 53 (Joey), retired at the Hawthorne. Pick up: in second race.' The 125cc McMenemy Honda had suffered a cold seizure. One more strip of tape would probably have done the job, but that's racing. He was picked up after the 125 race by a travelling marshal in a car collecting riders for the afternoon event. He might have been trying to impress 'our man' but it had to be said that he didn't exactly enjoy that ride and returned to the paddock somewhat less than pleased as well as angry with the morning's retirement. So the result of that 125 DNF was that Joseph Dunlop was running a somewhat higher adrenaline level than was usual before a race.

He left from the start of the Lightweight race, practically running on the stuff and the proverbial man on a mission. On the first lap, he was some 12 seconds ahead of James Courtney with Lofthouse a further eight behind him. Joey's lap was just short of 117mph from a standing start. He initially held that advantage as Lofthouse retired and Courtney was running hard, almost equalling lap times on lap four, but Joey ran out the winner, easing up and with a 25 second advantage. That was pure vintage Dunlop.

Joey was riding an unfamiliar V & M Honda in Wednesday's 600 Supersport race. John Harris had provided the 600 contender for the previous four years but the bike was getting long in the tooth. Jack Valentine of V & M Racing made Joey an offer of one of his 1995 bikes that he couldn't refuse; he partnered Ian Duffus on an identical bike.

The 600 Supersport race is always competitive, this year looked even more so after practice in which Joey had placed seventh, but with just a few seconds separating the top men everything looked possible. It has to be said though, it was a class in which Joey had never looked like winning, even though he had won the Irish 600 Championship in 1993.

The race now carried the title of 'Junior TT,' a reflection of the growing importance of the class, recognised by the manufacturers and the Isle of Man Tourist Board. In the paddock I'd inquired if he fancied his chances for this one. 'I'll tell you by Ballacraine whether we've got a race,' he responded just before joining the waiting machine on the start line.

However, Joey's fourth place was in fact his best placing in the class, won from the front by Duffus as Phillip McCallen broke the lap record in the closing stages to briefly snatch the lead before crashing out at the Waterworks. 'It was quite a steady ride though the wind was bad over The Mountain. It was a great run with Steve Ward together for most of the way. Then Phillip came by. No complaints and I quite enjoyed myself,' was his cryptic comment after the event.

With Phillip not on the grid in the Senior race due to commitments in Italy, it looked as though it was down to Joey to bear the brunt of the challenge to Honda from a trio of thundering Ducatis. Sure enough at the end of lap two, Joey's four led the bellowing Dukes of Duffus, Simon Beck and Rob Holden. He'd just a two second lead. With Davy in the pit as usual, Joey's stop was excellent and he left with the RC45 pawing the air to grab an extra second. 'Was that a good stop?' commented a satisfied Wood as Joey extended his lead.

Joey aboard the Castrol Honda pictured in Parliament Square. He went on to lose a titanic battle with Phillip McCallen.

Parliament Square in bright sunshine brought out the crowds to see Joey on the 250 in 1996.

Now Joey really got down to work and with the time gained in the pits he stretched his lead to 18 seconds over Ian Duffus. The first four were all averaging over 120mph at the end of lap two. The racing was certainly competitive - fast and furious would be a better description. 'It was a grand race,' said commentator Fred Clarke waxing lyrical over the PA. Holden then slipped off exiting Governor's Bridge and Beck's Peachurst Ducati's clutch was wilting as Nick Jefferies annexed third spot.

Joey won that race easing up to win a record 53rd Replica and a nineteenth victory. He promised to come back and try for a 20th in the post-race interview. He had averaged 119.11mph and his next pursuers, Duffus, Ward and Jefferies had all lapped over 121mph in their vain pursuit. The winning margin was still 33 seconds. 'The wind was a bit strong and you had to be careful not to run out of road. I'll have to get some more practice on the big bikes,' quipped 'The Man' after the race.

There had been the usual hurly-burly of the Irish season that year and there were some notable skirmishes with up-and-coming James Courtney and almost an equal number of wins by each of them. The Ulster was one of Joey's best. True, James had won the 125 but then Joey scored two convincing 250 wins setting fastest laps on each occasion. It was in the first Superbike race that Joey once more turned the clock back. In scoring a clear win and fastest lap against class opposition, many held that he was riding as well as anyone had ever seen from the man who was by now a 'veteran's veteran.'

After taking in the 600 race in which he placed seventh, it really did seem that Joey was asking too much from himself trying to compete in all classes and the second Superbike race would have been his sixth that day. He didn't start. 'I didn't go out in the last race. I was brave and tired and the 750s are hard to hold on to. If you're going to go at that speed, you'd better not be that tired,' said Joey. While all the old ability was clearly in evidence, perhaps even Joey could not ignore the passing of the years. But a treble win at that time of life and after a double at the TT! What could one say, how much more could there be to come?

1996: another notch on the Dunlop walking stick

This would not be a good year for Joseph Dunlop. He didn't exactly shine on the Irish circuits, and a crash in Latvia would ruin his European campaign. But on the 21st anniversary of his first TT ride, he would clock up his 21st win in the Isle of Man TT.

Season 1996 began with Joey involved in the usual rough and tumble of Irish racing and he opened his victory score at the Cookstown 100. The day had started slightly damp from light rain in practice but seemed to be clearing until there was almost a dry line all round. This was a fine start for Joey's first race of the season as I watched him head the pack off the line and lead it round the first corner. Leading all the way through he opened his victory score, extending it lap by lap. The few fine drops of drizzle gradually increased and things were that little bit more difficult for the 250 race in which he came round in ninth and pulled through to finish in fourth place. For the big race of the day he wheeled out the RC45 in worsening conditions to tour home tenth, blessed with more BHP than could be applied to the tarmac safely.

In fact that win on the 125 was the only one in several meetings before the TT where practice week for Joey was par for the course; steady rather than spectacular. Almost as usual, the RC45 was being somewhat recalcitrant in that the ideal suspension settings for the job were proving elusive; duplicating the 1995 settings should have been straightforward but wasn't; racing is still not an exact science and the RC45 sometimes defied

Eyes fixed firmly on the business in hand during the 250 race of 1996.

logic. The 250 was performing better and Joey had been third on the leader board in Wednesday evening's practice. The 125 had managed 104mph but the man was still searching for more. The races would tell. Joey like everyone else was suffering as a result of the lost practice sessions due to the bad weather.

The TT Formula I race start was delayed an hour as the weather still proved to be fickle with showers working their way across The Island. With wet patches still expected to be around, machines were, in the main, fitted with hand cut slicks. Joey's was similarly equipped but on the first lap he'd noted that conditions were rapidly improving and reckoned that if he could get slicks on before the others he'd have a real advantage.

McCallen had the lead from Duffus; Jefferies was next, then Joey who could be seen to be charging. First time past the start line McCallen led by six seconds, but Joey streaked into the pits and shouted for a slick shod rear wheel. Disaster; the pit crew expecting Joey in at the end of the second lap were unprepared and did not have the wheel ready, so Joey's chances were blown from there on. He departed in haste for another lap before his scheduled stop but was now over a minute behind and settled down for a steady ride, but even so that was quite enough to enable him to gradually climb up the leader board as front runners struck trouble. Seventh after losing a minute could not be that bad and with Phillip winning and Derek Young 13th, Joey shared another team prize; the MRRC of Ireland.

What should have been Monday's race programme actually took place on the Tuesday as Mona's fickle weather intervened. However, in fine weather the phenomenon that is Joey Dunlop continued to roll as he recorded his 20th win, in a 'nip and tuck' 250 race. Initially Phillip McCallen had looked to be the man who might deny him his 20th TT victory as they completed the second lap a couple of seconds apart, with Jim Moodie chasing hard in contention.

This time, Joey's pit stop delivered the goods as he started on into the third lap with a 14-second lead. But then Phillip's challenge started to fade; he had been riding so hard that he had worn a hole in an exhaust, taking the edge off the motor. Now it was Moodie's turn to tilt at the Master of the Mountain. He closed a little through the third and into the last lap Jim made his effort and ate into Joey's lead second by second. Alerted by his signallers, Joey proved to be quicker from Glen Helen to Ramsey and hauled back three seconds, but The Mountain was Moodie's ace; previous times had showed him to be quicker than Joey.

At Ramsey Hairpin for the last time the 'Ballymoney Bullet' (as commentator Fred Clarke christened him) led by 11 seconds and we in the

A bungled pit stop in the '96 FI race at the TT cost Joey one minute and put him well down the field.

pits waited to see what cards Lady Luck would deal. Moodie was flying and reducing that lead; riding like a man possessed as Joey crossed the line. In the packed grandstand time seem to stand still. There was a 50-second starting difference between them and the stopwatches counted down with the crowd almost silent. But Joey it was and Jim mused on the time that back markers had cost him and what might have been - so it might well, but in the Isle of Man almost more than anywhere else, Lady Luck deals the cards and Joey had actually won by just six point seven seconds. 'That'll do,' said Joey with a broad, tired grin.

At the prize giving for the 250s the crowds had as usual taken the roof off with applause when Joey mounted the stage steps to where the ACU and Manx officials sat in front of serried ranks of Replica trophies. Chairman of the Auto Cycle Union Bill Rawlinson recalled that occasion as he was presenting the trophies for the race. 'Joey brought his family up onto the stage. I had the privilege of presenting the trophy to his youngest daughter. Joey was over the moon and it was a proud moment for me as well.'

Even if he didn't win the races, Joey was always the centre of media attention. Things didn't always go to plan but he was never one to complain.

21 for Joey's 21st TT

After repeated postponements during the day as clouds swirled around the Mountain, the 125 race was reduced to two laps and started some six hours late. Joey must have been favourite and was riding an unfamiliar No 18 but he was pushed all the way by Gavin Lee. Lee actually led by two seconds at the end of a lap, which eliminated top contender Denis McCullough as his Honda, seized at Brandywell. So Joey had it all to do and by Ramsey Hairpin last time 'over the top' Joey led by just 0.3s. In a sprint over The Mountain in clouds that almost spoiled the race, Dunlop clinched his 21st TT victory by just 3.8 seconds and on his 21st year of TT racing.

Joey's race week was concluded by something of a meteoric sprint through to second place in Friday's Senior race. On the first lap he'd reported trouble with the carburation but the fuel management system shrugged off the initial 'glitch' and by the end of lap one, Joey was back on the pace, but now having been reported as down in eighth.

For this race Joey was clearly serious as he was playing the strategy that had won him the previous year's Senior when he made the six laps without taking on fresh rubber - so that there could be no hiccups to delay him. He gradually picked his way through the field and by the fifth lap he was within striking distance of team mate Nick Jefferies and as he said after the race: 'I just kept my head down under the screen. I knew what I had to do from my pit signals and went for it. I had several big moments on the last lap as the tyre was now going off.' That part of the race plan worked as he snatched second place from Jefferies by just 1.8 seconds and clocked a lap at 121.89mph; his fastest ever TT lap. So while McCallen had made the fastest lap of the race, one had to wonder how close the challenge might have been but for that first-lap problem.

So after one more victorious TT, Joey as usual took in the Steam Packet races immediately afterwards and scored a win on the 250 and fourth on the 125 before resuming his attempt to retain his Pure Roads title and departed to Latvia for the next round in Riga. Things would not go according to plan though, after wins on the 125 and 750, Joey 'lost' the front wheel on the 250 and crashed quite heavily. He actually broke his lower shoulder blade - more of a fracture, and the finger that had been trapped under the bike while it bounced on the road was somewhat mangled and would require a skin and tendon graft. Lucky for Joey, the organiser of the Series, Billy Nutt, was at the meeting and immediately arranged a flight home for him where he could receive the expert ministrations at Ulster's Royal Victoria Hospital.

Joey then took something of a recuperation by taking the family to Portugal for a break and to let the graft settle down as it was troubling him. But the next event he turned out for in the roads series was the final round at Fromberg in Germany after a nine-week layoff. However, the 'comeback' was a little premature as the injuries were still not quite properly healed and he settled for a sixth on the 250.

He was then scheduled to appear at Scarborough for the parade of former Champions to celebrate the circuit's 50th anniversary. He is listed as finishing in tenth in the 125 race while on the 250 the clutch chose the moment to self-destruct. Joey did, however, join the parade of former champions on a borrowed and mellifluous sounding Honda K4.

After the racing season was over, Joey once more felt the need to journey to Bosnia and Romania and this time it was just to renew acquaintances and to see how his friends in the orphanages were progressing. Not in his van this time; that proved to be an unfortunate choice. 'I was heading to Bosnia and Romania before Christmas just to see the people again but I lost third gear on the car as I went through Austria. I stayed in Austria for a week, it was minus 15 degrees there. I coaxed the car back home without third gear. I also went to Imola to visit the place where Senna was killed. I'll probably go back to Bosnia, Albania and Romania some day.'

The crowds hold their breath as McCallen and Dunlop battle it out in the mid-day sun.

Billy Nutt on Joey

Billy Nutt, organiser of the North West 200 and Ulster, while playing a significant part in the resurgence of road racing in Ireland himself throughout the last couple of decades, is quick to acknowledge the debt owed to riders like Joey who have brought the fans back to levels envied by any UK organiser.

'Joey as a man is so hard to sum up,' mused Billy. 'Although I've known him for something like 25 years from the days when he used to have those

Simply THE BEST!

great battles with Raymond McCullough, the Armoy Armada v the Dromara Destroyers, he still continues to amaze me the way that he does the things that he does.

'It seems to be something of a public myth that Joey is not well organised and usually turns up late for meetings. Those stories simply are not true. He does turn up at meetings with little time to spare but his bikes are well prepared and ready to go and Estonia would be a good example. I was waiting for him at the docks and he just drove up in his Mercedes van by himself, the van loaded up with his three bikes. The organisers had kept on asking when the mechanics would be arriving. He just unloaded his bikes and won four races that day.'

'On his day, Joey is unbeatable. I remember when he proved that; three years ago at the Ulster, Phillip (McCallen) expected to run away with the Superbike race but Joey had other ideas and just beat him in a memorable last lap. Then there was the time he outsmarted Roger Marshall right on the last lap; Roger wasn't too pleased either.'

'There is no doubt that Joey and the FI Series were a big factor in helping to keep the Ulster alive in the '80s. While we no longer have FI and the event is good right now, in the future something like the Pure Roads series is intended to go some way to keep up the interest.

'Joey is very well known in all the countries where the series takes place and attracts a big following in Belgium - Mettet, Fromberg in Germany, Tallin - Estonia, Riga - Latvia, and the Ulster and North West 200. In the face of Superbike and Grands Prix, we organisers are getting together to generate publicity for road racing and promote events in which hundreds of riders take part, not just the 30 in Grands Prix.

'I've got to know Joey far more in the last couple of years with the involvement in the European Pure Roads Championship. He portrays quite a different personality to the general public from the real man. He is really very intelligent and knows exactly what he has to do and just gets on with it, on his own terms. He is unique, they'll never be another like him.

SEGA
SATURN

Twenty-third TT win

1997-1998

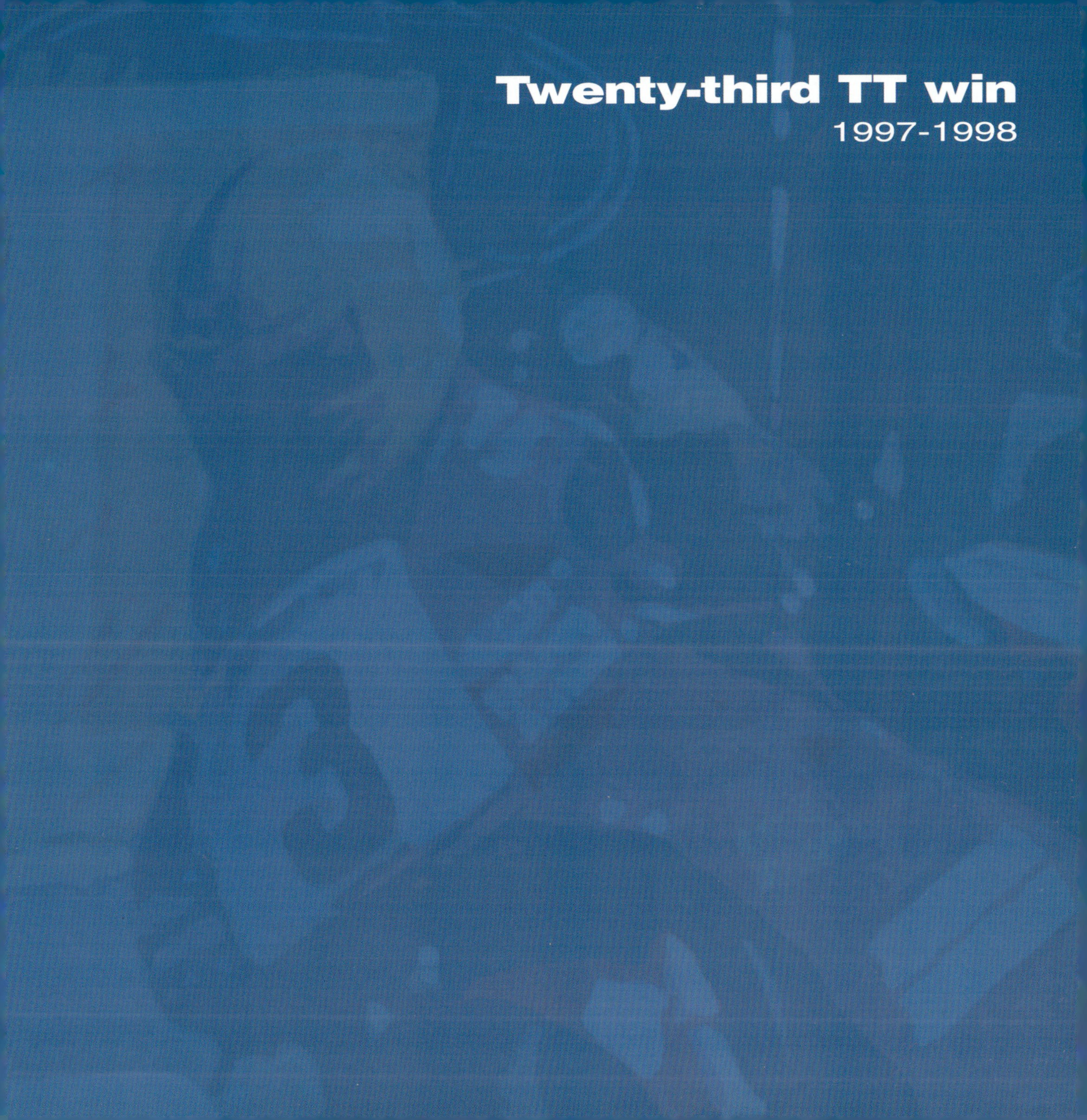

Applause for Joey at the Gooseneck as he tips the RC45 to the limits.

One might have been forgiven for thinking that after 23 years racing, some of the raw enthusiasm might have been fading. However, that thought was clearly somewhat wide of the mark when Joey spent some days during the winter at the Honda Race headquarters in Lincolnshire working on the RC45 he would ride in the TT. If that were not sufficient, then he was so enthused at the thought of riding Honda's latest race bike, the GP500 vee-twin, that he arrived at Bishopscourt on a cold March evening before the official practice day. He slept in his van overnight to be ready to 'give it a crack' as soon as possible in the morning.

A week later saw Joey take the new bike to the line at Aghadowey for a race test on the NSR-V500 two-stroke at the first meeting. On that short circuit the 500 would pop a wheelie almost every time that Joey opened the throttle; the front wheel just would not stay in contact with the tarmac and he had to settle for sixth and eighth places while learning the handling characteristics of the bike. The power characteristics of the 500 grand prix two-stroke twin were described by some as like a switch; on or off, but the real problem was the power-to-weight ratio; lots of the former and not so much more than a 250 for the latter.

This is far less of a problem on Grands Prix circuits but on courses where you need to feed power on through a section, it does pose particular problems. The machine's whole 'raison d'étre' is simply to provide a power-to-weight ratio that gives the next best thing to Grand Prix four cylinder machine performance by employing around 135bhp coupled to the weight and bulk of a 250. And in fact it really is little bigger and heavier and as Joey said at the TT, 'it just pulls your arms off.'

However, things were different in the 125 races. In the first, there were five riders in a 'freight train' in and out of each other's slipstreams and Joey had his turn at the front. But at the end of the ten laps he was fifth after something of a meteoric scrap in a race won by Chris Richardson. While Denis McCullough was second, it's worth recording that third place man Paul Robinson is Joey's nephew, son of brother-in-law Mervyn Robinson. This merely served to wet Joey's appetite for the next race on the McMenemy 125 in which he just slipped up a gear to snatch a foot here and there to win by eight machine lengths, and at a meeting where there was no prize money either. He still liked racing just for the sheer fun of competition.

Mettet - Belgium: back on the roads again

The Pure Roads of Europe Street Series started again at Mettet and Joey put his marker down as wanting to win the series once more. Local hero Marc Fissette and 22 years Joey's junior, added Dunlop to his already impressive competition record by beating him into second spot on the 250. In a very busy and competitive day, there was also a third on the 125 behind Rudy de Haes and Serge Julin and 12th place on John Harris's 600.

Back at the North West, riding John's CBR, Joey had been having a pretty good ride and was actually up to fifth place. However, while involved in a close dice, he was taken up the slip road by another rider who had decided that he couldn't make the corner but was inside him at the time; it's the sort of thing that happens at the 'NW.' In the fiercely competitive 125 and 250 fields, he also scored 10th on the 125 and 9th on the 250 as riders nipped in and out of each others slipstreams down the long straights. You can go from the first three to last of 12 with a missed gear change at the North West.

He was out on the NSR-V500 again as a further pre-TT shakedown. Finishing fifth it might not have looked that good, given the machine's performance in last years Grands Prix where it achieved rostrum positions; but it was better than the placing suggested. Captured on Ulster TV, the bike hadn't actually looked that fast, just going along with the leading 750s in the race. However, this was largely due to the fact that the gearbox internal ratios left a large gap between fifth and sixth and when changing up from one to the other, the engine would be almost out of the power-band. Alternative ratios were not yet available.

TT 1997

After a fairly uneventful practice session in brilliant weather, the Saturday's Formula I race programme opener initially looked as though the favourite, Phillip McCallen, just might be in for a surprise. It's been said by many that you can never rule Joey out in a TT race and at the first commentary point he was actually leading on time. As a retrospective note, Nick Jefferies had crashed his 600 in practice and was a non-starter for the race. Joey was given his 750 and he was most happy with it with a standing start lap at over 122mph. He was running hard and very fast with his race-face firmly in place that day.

However, Phillip would not be denied. He was in his almost customary leading position by Ramsey Hairpin and would not be headed again, though it is worth noting that Phillip had a full, world superbike spec machine for the job and the potential extra 20bhp was almost being offset by an inspired Dunlop. In spite of the power deficit, Joey was holding a strong second and still in with every chance of being in that place on the rostrum at the very least; until the pit stop time at the end of the second lap. However, once more fate took a hand. As Phillip's filler cap proved awkward to refit, costing him precious extra seconds in his stop, Joey suffered a complete disaster.

First, he stalled the engine in the stop box and then paddled the bike into his nearby pit in neutral, where the wheel changing operation went

pear-shaped. The rider needs to keep the rear brake applied so that the wheel nut can be removed, but the bike was in neutral. The QD wheel had heated up to the extent that it had jammed on its splines and just would not be removed and the mechanics had to sweat and swear to get it off. Then the rear wheel nut chose this moment not to slip nicely onto its threads and the whole operation cost Joey over 70 seconds and the race was effectively lost. Now somewhat disheartened and out of contention, Joey finished the race in sixth place.

Speaking after the race, Joey confessed that the sheer physical effort of completing the race had left him feeling pretty tired, on top of which the incident in the pits had left him ready to pack up altogether. But that would

No where was he more at home than on the TT circuit. This shot by Ian Kerr captures the magic of Dunlop with the Isle of Man hills in the background; a classic shot of a classic rider at the very top of his profession.

Joey on his way to his twenty-first win in the 1997 Lightweight TT. He was a master of the lightweights and makes easy work of tipping the 250 into Sulby Bridge.

all soon change with the Lightweight race. This was another battle with McCallen and there was plenty of other top class opposition led by lap record holder Ian Lougher, to name but one.

It turned out to be something of an epic initial two laps as Joey and Phillip jousted at over 116mph average laps and at the end of the first they were separated by a mere one point two seconds. The old Master held the lead from he who would presume to take his mantle and at the end of the second, the pace of the scrap was red hot and times for the two laps were dead level at 116.71mph.

Now it would be that Phillip made a tactical error as he decided to change his rear wheel after the initial two laps. He had been running a softer compound rear boot with the idea that he would be able to make up for the time it took to change the wheel by faster lap speeds and still come out on top. 'I knew that Phillip was on a softer tyre but wasn't sure if he would change it or not. I knew that if he did, it would cost him a lot of time,' commented Joey after the race. In fact Joey went into the third lap with an 18 second lead and the race was virtually won. Lady Luck was riding Joey's pillion on this occasion.

However, Phillip set out determined to retrieve the time it took to take on fresh rubber and riding like a man possessed, went storming into the right hand entry to Quarry Bends, but at such a speed that the front tyre would refuse to do his bidding. As the front end 'washed out' McCallen pirouetted down the road at well over 120mph and he was so very lucky not to hit anything hard and sustained only bumps and abrasions. He walked away with no more than a right hand that bore real signs of heavy bruising. The chase for Joey's lead now fell to Ian Lougher. He was able to run out a comfortable winner by some 47 seconds, though even at the reduced rate of progress, the rear tyre had given of its best and he said that he'd had slides on the last lap.

Victory number 22 in his 22nd year of TTs

It would have been reasonable, given his record, for Joey to start as favourite for the Ultra Lightweight race and though he'd not really shone in practice, Dunlop's best efforts are always reserved for the main event. Practice times for him are not only largely academic, but he's known to sprint from

place to place and tour the rest; a tactic that tends to disguise form. In the event though, the 125 had lacked horses all through the week and even a new barrel and piston, flown in the previous day and run in at Jurby Airfield before the race, still failed to produce sufficient gee gees to get into the hunt. A lowly tenth was the result in the race won by Ian Lougher in which he set a new lap record at 109.25mph. A footnote to the race was the superb third place achieved by brother Robert on the O'Kane Honda after being refused permission to ride in the North West 200 for medical reasons on his long comeback trail from that awful TT crash.

A 120mph lap on a 600 by winner Ian Simpson, timed from Ramsey to Ramsey commentary point, testified to just how incredibly competitive the Junior race has become. One has to doubt that even a fit McCallen could have beaten him, as it was he was still nursing the bruises from his Lightweight crash. It was a race in which Joey clocked his fastest lap for the class ever, at 118.34mph, to finish a good fifth, and that time was on his last lap too as he grew more accustomed to his road (treaded) tyres.

The Senior was notable for one small fact; it was the race in which Joey didn't ride under his almost legendary Number 3. He actually raced carrying Number 5 on his RC45. As something of a radical change of policy by the Auto Cycle Union this year, places on the grid for the Senior were allocated to the fastest 70 timed riders in practice in the 250, 600 and FI classes; Joey had clocked the fifth fastest time of the week.

In the one lap practice session after Wednesday's races, Joey took out the 500 vee-twin to make his decision on which bike to ride on the Friday, but although fitted with new gear ratios, the power characteristics of the motor were still radically 'on-off.' 'It's pulling my arms out,' said Joey. He was in any case being treated at the time for what was described as 'tennis elbow,' and the five hundred's vicious power delivery was beginning to stir up the old shoulder injury sustained in that bad Brands Hatch crash nearly a decade ago.

It was therefore an easy decision for him to elect to ride the 750. With its smooth power delivery as the big plus, the fact of it being a lot heavier meant that it rode the bumps better. The 500 was only a few kilos heavier than a 250 and would rear up on the back wheel so much that he had to back off the throttle where the 750 could be kept driving. Practice times had been little different on the two bikes, but it was simply the case that the 750 was an easier ride. As it turned out though, the Senior was simply one of those where Joey hadn't really got his race-face on, and a steady rather than an ultimately competitive ride saw him finish in seventh place. The race was dominated by Phillip with Jim Moodie fighting the other 500-V to a creditable second spot.

Back on Irish soil and on Dundalk's tight road course Joey had something of an eventful meeting, being nearly 'nerfed off' twice. It was at the start of the 250 that Phil Reid tumbled and his cart-wheeling bike hit Joey's, resulting in quite a melee. On the restart, Derek Young actually looped his bike and Joey was bumped once more. Next, a week later at the County Louth races and in a busy day, Joey finished 3rd in the open race, 5th in the 250 and 7th in the hard-fought 125.

The Dundrod 150 is a regular for Joey where the going suits him well. However, the 1997 meeting was staged in somewhat indifferent weather

A shot that says, 'This is the Isle of Man'. Ramsey provides the backcloth for this picture of Joey on the 125 as he heads up to Guthrie's Memorial.

and it would be tyre choices and stones that were the deciding factors. Joey was still persevering with the 500 vee-twin and took it out in practice which went well enough. But, come the race and it boiled up before the off and the reason proved to be that a stone had punctured the radiator and there was precious little coolant left in the system. It could have been worse in the heat of a race if it had seized.

This traditional Quarter Bridge shot catches Joey just as he is about to apply some serious power.

Out on John Harris's 600 again it looked for a while, indeed near to the end of the race, that he would win, but then the CBR slowed and he finished the race in a cloud of steam; the pebble-through-the-radiator syndrome had struck again. The result was a sixth place.

Joey then went off to Estonia and would come directly to the Isle of Man just in time to compete in the Southern 100. In the paddock before practice I caught him fitting a new chain to the 500 for a brief word: 'How was Estonia?' I enquired. 'It was great,' said Joey. 'I won the big race on the last lap on the 500.' 'Isn't the 500 like a switch to ride?' 'No,' he said, 'Its not too bad really,' to shatter another bit of Paddock gossip; that is until Davy Wood later confided that new pipes had made life a little easier. With a double win in the 125 and 250 events, Joey came away with a clean sweep and haul of points that would ensure another Series win.

The Southern 100 saw something of an unusual event for a Honda RC45 when Joey actually had an engine blow up and had to 'file it' for the rest of the meeting. Declining to ride the 500, he fielded the 250 in the big races, but there's no real substitute for that many cubes. In the combined 600/250 event, Joey scored first in class and 6th overall. But in the keenly contested 125 events, Dunlop the younger continued his return to fitness with two fine wins as Joey chased home Gavin Lee in the second race for fifth. Then on to August 3rd when the Mid-Antrim 150 took place and, out on his 250 again, he took fourth in a race won easily by Gary Dynes, who himself scored fourth in the 125, beating Joey into fifth.

The Ulster Grand Prix saw Joey being crowned 'Man of the Meeting' as the he rode four machines and scratched as hard as anyone out there. In particular, the 250 saw Joey scrap with old Mettet adversary, young Marc Fissette, this time turning the tables in what was certainly a thrilling finish. They scrapped nose to tail throughout the race and Fissette made some passing moves where Joey later confessed he'd not thought it possible. As the saying goes, it went right down to the wire with the result only being decided by Joey coming out of Marc's slipstream across the line to win by 0.3s.

In the first Superbike race, Joey was getting to grips with the vee-twin 500 and scored a good third spot in the race that counted for the European series and, when all the scores were added up, he won all three classes; Superbike, 250 and 125.

An end of season, something of a holiday, visit to Macau again, saw Joey take the 500 with him. As it turned out it wasn't such a good idea with a 13th place finish, rushing through avenues of Armco, right on the edge of the circuit. Joey put the result down to the bike developing little power under 8,000, making life very difficult on the sinuous track.

Just in case anyone thought that the fire was beginning to wane after almost countless years of competition, as preparation for the 1998 season, Joey departed the UK's miserable winter for the guaranteed good weather in Australia. The seven weeks that he spent there were to ensure that the man who was quite old enough to be the father of many of his up-and-coming challengers, started his season just as super-fit as a 47-year-old racer can be. As something of a footnote, back in 1986, Joey had expressed the idea of emigrating to OZ, and this and subsequent visits, reveal a little more of the 'free spirit' within the calm exterior.

It would be the traditional season opener at Cookstown where he opened his score and, as the meeting was reported in the April 29th issue of Motor Cycle News, 'Golden Oldies off to a Flyer;' the other flier was Bob Jackson. Commencing his 29th racing season, Joey won the 250 race, easily escaping from his pursuers and at the flag Denis McCullough was eight seconds in arrears. On the 125, Joey lost the race for fourth place to younger brother Robert in an event won by Gary Dynes. Joey had sustained damage to the 125s radiator from the many stones on the course, something complained of by many competitors. Indeed, after the race, Joey was quoted as saying: 'The flying stones gave me bleeding knuckles.' After which he put the 500 back in the van; it was too precious to risk damaging it with the North West and the TT in mind.

A week later at the Tandragee, the fitness earned in OZ went 'pear-shaped' as Joey lost the 125 over a series of bumps while dicing for the lead with Owen McNally and Robert. Race reports listed his injuries as a cracked collarbone and pelvis, broken bone in his right hand and somewhat shredded 'ring finger' on his left. Subsequently, part of the finger was amputated.

In the Jerry Kelly programme on Ulster TV on the 22nd May, Joey and Robert were interviewed showing their various injuries. Robert had sustained a broken leg from a heavy fall at University Corner at the North West meeting, taken out by another competitor and having collided with a post. Joey was almost cheerful during the show, displaying the amputated stump and vowing to be in the Island for Honda's 50th birthday celebrations. Even Robert reckoned to be there, wearing his new 'breathing' plaster-cast and thought that he too stood a chance of passing the medical.

While non-starting at the North West, Joey straight-away announced his intention of being at the TT and, while the pundits doubted that he would be able to pass the medical before the race, I couldn't believe that the little man from Ballymoney would once more defy all the experts to grace Honda's 50th anniversary meeting with his presence on the grid.

Incredible is just about the only word to describe the Dunlop brothers performances at the TT. Both were passed fit to ride at the last moment by

Chief Medical Officer David Stevens. Both astounded their legions of fans on the Island. Robert straight-away topped the practice leader board and knocked seconds off the lap record. From the start he made the race his own to record his fifth 125cc victory.

Joey however, did not start quite so decisively. After the first day's practice he pulled out of the FI and Senior races on the RC45 and the Junior on John Harris's 600; he even confided to Bob McMillan that the 250 ride was doubtful as well. Indeed it wasn't until the end of the week that he thought he'd ride anything. The injuries just couldn't be ignored.

The weather for the Lightweight race wasn't just bad; it was dreadful. But it might have been made for Joey. Below par in many ways, not the least in sheer physical strength in his hands, the 'stump' on his left hand plus scarce healed bones in the right, would have persuaded most men to non-start. But the conditions did not place a premium on strength and as the rain came down, Joey knew he had a chance after all. The fact of him making the fastest lap of the race at just over the ton on the first lap tells a story in itself. Already over half a minute in front of John McGuinness, the rain that had recommenced at the start of the race really opened the sluice gates; a third of the field was lapping at less than 80 mph.

The 1997 600 TT was a red hot affair both on and off the track. Joey swoops into The Bungalow ahead of Derek Young.

Man and machine in perfect unison, Joey aboard the 250 at the 1997 TT.

Into the second lap and the organisers cut the race from its already-shortened three laps to two by which time Joey was easing up towards the chequered flag. His choice of tyres had in any case been crucial; heavy patterned intermediates. Like similar veteran Bob Jackson in second place, course knowledge had been the other factor. Both had used their supreme road racing skills to overcome conditions so bad that the rest of the day's programme was abandoned. For Dunlop it presented him with a fifth consecutive win in that race, on a day that could well be seen as especially made for him. On the rostrum with three of the children, he positively enjoyed the cheering crowd's adulation. Speaking to Norrie Whyte after the race, Joey said: 'I doubt that I could have hung onto the 250 for four laps in the dry. I'm trussed up like a Christmas turkey with strapping on my injured collarbone, so I'm a bit stiff with all the wet and cold.'

As Robert romped away with the Ultra Lightweight race win, Joey had still managed a first lap at 103mph giving him ninth place; it was a position he held until the end and a hard-earned, in that physical condition, Silver Replica to end one more TT.

After the TT and his historic 23rd win on Honda's 50th birthday of their race debut in the Island, Joey announced a holiday to get back on the road to fitness and took the family off to Portugal again.

It was back to business for the Mid-Antrim 150 at Clough, where both Joey and brother Robert suffered the same problem with seizures on their 125s. Getting out the 500 twin earned a fourth in the open race as James Courtney was dominant on his RC45 and Gary Dynes did the business in the 250 race where another fourth was recorded. A week later, Courtney was still the man to beat at the Kells meeting in Co. Meath. Joey brought the twin home to eighth, though a third in the 250 event was some consolation as the 125 race was a botched start with some competitors getting away while others, including both Dunlops, waited for the flag.

For the third weekend in a row Joey gave the 500 an outing, scoring seventh in the open race at Glaslough on the Sunday before going on to the Ulster GP at Dundrod with the vee-four. In the first Superbike race, Hondas filled the first five places with Ian Simpson to the fore and Joey sixth, followed by 10th in the second and 12th in the 250. For the last Irish road-race meeting of the year, the results at Killalane showed him with just a sixth place result on the 250.

A packed house marvels at Joey in the 1996 Isle of Man Senior TT.

Nick Jefferies on Joey; fellow Honda Team Member 1995-97.

'He has the respect of the riders, officials, and most importantly, the crowds, and they do love him. Perhaps some of our 'stars' could do with a long look at Joey's style, they could learn a lot.

1995 was my first year riding an RC45 in the Isle of Man. It was early in practice week and suspension settings were still being refined to suit individual team members. Joey had followed me and thought my bike handled OK; his not so good.

So I told him how mine was set up (drastically different to his). He tried my settings on his own and came back into the paddock afterwards. I thought: 'Here goes all my credibility and lo and behold, he put his arm around me and in a broad Irish accent, indicated that it was a 'friggin different bike.'

There was a big grin all over his face and from that point onwards we have spoken more together in six months than we had in the previous 20 years and in fact I have the odd blush when he has commented on some of our dices together.'

The orphanage runs

Joey Dunlop is a religious man and his humanitarian trips overseas were all done with the blessing of the church.

The story of the first drive to Romania, transporting food and clothing to an orphanage, received little coverage at the time, other than comment of the fact in Motor Cycle News. But further drives to Bosnia and Albania did come to the recognition of 'the establishment' and led, together with his TT exploits, to the award of the OBE. It is surely deeds like this that really reveal the heart of the man. They would be described by many as heroic.

To describe the man as a hero to his face would embarrass him; it's a concept he would not relate to. The fact of driving 3,000 miles alone across deeply troubled areas of Europe in conditions so cold that diesel fuel sometimes froze, is one that epitomises a single-mindedness of purpose only demonstrated by exceptional people who undertake tasks that many would consider foolhardy. They just do it.

I first uncovered the story and carried some details of it in the April '92 issue of the magazine Motorcycle Sport. At the time, John Harris was sponsoring both Joey and myself on CBR 600s. Through him I'd heard of the details and others filled in the gaps.

It seems that a nurse in a Romanian orphanage had written home to her mother in the town of Ballymoney, requesting that Mother send a food parcel as the children she was caring for were becoming somewhat more than undernourished. Mother wanted to do just that but found that postal costs alone would be more than double the cost of the food. And it seemed doubtful, given the potential problems en-route and vagaries of the postal system, that the food would ever reach its destination.

In a small town like Ballymoney, it didn't take long for the knowledge of the problem to become public. Joey, like anyone else watching the TV news that daily depicted the plight of children in that area, wanted to do something to help. I suppose we all did, but he just volunteered to drive out there in his race van to deliver the goods personally without so much as a thought of the potential consequences of being caught in a war zone. From there on the Irish spirit took over as the word got onto local radio and television. Chapels and churches, clubs and local businesses came forward to support the project and the goods poured in.

Now at that time, Joey was scheduled to take in a few weeks in South Africa on a pre-season racing and training programme and something of a holiday. This he quickly cancelled as the project gathered pace. A local haulage company offered to supply the many gallons of diesel required for the long journey, through Continental suppliers used by their own lorries wherever the routes could be made to coincide.

Even the local VAT office entered into the spirit of the exercise by rating anything to do with the business at zero. Another well-wishing transport company, gave his van a complete overhaul free of charge.

In an interview for the 1996 TT programme, Joey said that just because you are taking humanitarian supplies and are strictly a neutral body, does not ensure that you have a free passage. On one occasion, on the way back from Albania, he was arrested at gunpoint as it was felt that his documentation was not in order. 'They wanted me to pay £25 to cross the check-point but I wouldn't pay them. However, I carried plenty of racing stickers and motorcycle papers and gave them some of those to break the ice. And as luck would have it, the Chief of Police turned out to be a motorsport fan and we got on so well that he wrote me a letter allowing me to continue,' said Joey.

On another occasion, when he arrived at the church in Albania, he described how the armed guards charged him £10 per night to stay overnight. 'I parked the van in the helicopter landing area and was forced to stay there from 19.30 to 07.30 the next day. They let me have a shower, but I was escorted all the way by armed soldiers. I was a bit scared. Although I live in Northern Ireland, I live out in the country mostly away from the troubles, so seeing a gun still came as something of a shock. However, I'm pleased that I went on the trip and will probably go again. The children in those countries need help and I am only doing my bit.'

Arai
12

Racer resurgent

1999

The Dunlop plan for 1999 was, again, to start off really fit. So, like last year, it was back to OZ and let the warmth and sunshine to do their healing work. Returning from the Australian summer, Joey proved that it had done him a lot of good at the Easter Monday Kirkistown meeting. He just wheeled out the RC45 and blew the field away in the big race of the day. It would be a preface to performances in '99 that said that 'Father Time' would have to wait awhile yet before that famous yellow helmet would be retired.

The Cookstown meeting on April 24th was run on the new 'Orritor' course and, while the final results didn't show him too well placed, he was certainly making his presence felt. Away in the lead with Courtney in the final race of the day, Richard Britton tumbled and spread oil on the course, which terminated the day's proceedings. There'd been a fiercely competitive 125 race in which Joey had been in the thick of it along with brother Robert and finally finished in sixth place. Not since his 1993 season when he won the Irish 600 and Regal championships has Joey excelled on a 600 but in the Regal race he had sparred with Jason Griffiths among other notables in the pack chasing the leaders. The results record Jason 10th, Joey 11th.

In the North West 200, Ian Simpson crashed prior to the meeting, and, as the commentator put it, Joey was handed the Honda Britain RC45. However, he didn't even get the chance to practice on the Thursday evening as the weather was dreadful and while the small classes got out, the Superbike session was cancelled. Practice was marred by the fatal crash of Donny Robinson at Mill Road roundabout. He'd been prominent in leading the resurgence of Irish road racing in earlier days, frequently jousting with Joey, and had returned after a ten-year layoff, still showing all his old talent. Joey clearly felt the loss.

The first Superbike race was a cracker with David Jefferies taking his 1000cc R1 Yamaha to victory with the first five putting in laps at over 112mph. Joey ran home in seventh behind John McGuinness' vee-twin 500 GP Honda and Phillip McCallen, returning after a long layoff with injuries, also on another R1. A tenth on the 125, retirement on the 250, 11th on the 600, NS in the Junior and 2nd Superbikes, and it couldn't be said to be one of his more successful North West 200s. One might have been forgiven for thinking that he didn't look like a top man for the TT. However, this just goes to show that Joey should never be disregarded in any race on his favourite circuit, something said by several people who really know.

And so to TT 1999 - even faster!

Monday's opening evening session produced surprises for all those who might have thought that the veteran wee man was losing his motivation. It wasn't just that he topped the leader board on the 'tiddler' at over 106mph, it was the fact of taking the Honda Britain RC45 round at a blistering 119.30mph lap. He was 0.5 of a second behind Jim Moodie on the other works bike and with them both just a fraction behind top man Ian Duffus on a V&M R1 Yamaha.

Tuesday wasn't so good though. First the Superbike spec' RC45 broke a crankshaft, then the 250 seized before it, too, later broke its crank But philosophically Joey reckons: 'trouble in practice, good race.'

The FI race saw Joey put in an absolutely incredible performance in that he recorded his fastest ever TT lap, at over 123mph, after all those years competing over The Mountain course. It was though, at the cost of burning up his rear slick. This put paid to the usual tactic of not changing tyres, and the resultant long pit stop as the mechanics tardily changed the wheel left him 15 seconds in arrears as the leader, David Jefferies on an R1 Yamaha, held the lead. But Joey really gave his all on the last lap in pursuit of the flying Yamaha. He now carried all Honda's hopes with Moodie having retired. However, with the chips down, Jefferies went just a fraction faster to take the win. For Joey, a fastest lap on his 24th year - the man was amazing.

Monday's 250 race was not a good one for Joey. He and James Courtney had been riding closely together when, at Greeba Bridge on the first lap, James had a big 'off' when his Aprilia clipped the curb and it had looked very bad for James from where Joey had been sitting. Being good friends, it had taken the edge off his motivation, in spite of which he still 'toured' to a steady fifth place, averaging 114.48mph on the Payne-Honda.

Joey really had to be a favourite in the Ultra Lightweight but, getting no further than Ballacraine on the first lap, the commentator announced that Dunlop had stopped for adjustments and proceeded. He then stopped at his pit on lap one to clear what turned out to be a tank breather blocked by a trace of silicone sealant. Following the normal fill up,

and now quite out of contention, Joey nevertheless was determined to give his thousands of fans something to cheer for. He proceeded to crack in a final lap at over 109mph, just fractionally short of the record and the fastest lap of the race to finish in 27th place. Just what could one say. With absolutely nothing to be gained, he put in that quite incredible lap speed.

Joey has never really shone on a 600 in the Island, though fourth in 1995 can hardly be bad. Never really taking to treaded tyres, he nevertheless had a cracking ride on the Harris CBR after a race long dice with Adrian Archibald. Adrian had caught Joey at Sulby on the first lap having eliminated the ten second starting interval. They were still together at Signpost on the last lap with Adrian leading when Joey pulled out an ace to slip in front though he was still, of course, ten seconds back on time. They both cracked in a last lap at a 'smidgen' short of 119mph and that really did break new ground for the veteran from Ballymoney. Adrian said after the race: 'I caught him at Sulby on the first lap and stuck with him for the rest of the race. We had a great race, I passed Joey a few times but he kept passing me - I couldn't get rid of him.' As Joey saw it: 'I'm not very good on a 600 so I'm pleased with fifth place. I had a good race with Adrian, he was teaching me one or two things.' Truly the man is modest.

So now for the Senior. It has to be said that on this day, Jim Moodie looked to be unstoppable, putting in an opening lap that broke the record, leaving it at 124.45mph. However, that blistering lap was at the expense of going out on the second when great gaps could be seen in the rubber of his rear tyre. 'Himself' was, until then, running in third spot behind Jefferies and we, the watching thousands listening to the commentary, wondered whether it just might be Joey's day once more. It was not to be however, as Duffus speeded up. The first six men were all lapping at over 121mph though none would threaten Jefferies on his way to a historic treble for the week. Joey, in the interview afterwards, accounted himself well pleased with an enjoyable ride to fifth place, being caught towards the end by Lougher and Davies in spite of a last lap at 122.74mph.

Questioned by commentator Geoff Cannell in the paddock after the race as to whether this would be his last TT, Joey commented laconically: 'Oh, we'll have to think about that one when we get back.' It might have

Joey in the thick of the action with youngsters half his age. Here he leads Adrian Archibald and Chris Heath in the 1999, 600 Junior race.

been thought less than a successful TT for Joey, but given his speeds, he could still have made it 24 out of 24. And given his fastest ever lap after all this time, surely Joey would not consider retirement now.

The TT Festival fortnight ends with the Steam Packet races and with his appetite for racing after a solid fortnight's endeavors still unsatiated, Joey then went on to take the Packet races by storm. The truly remarkable talent of this man to master machines at opposite ends of the spectrum was emphasised when he won the first race, the 125 event, after a real tussle with Ian Lougher, by a tyre's width at the last gasp after coming from behind. Then, after a somewhat lethargic start on the RC45, he scooped up a new race record for the meeting at 104.89mph to overhaul Griffiths and Kiwi star Blair Degerholm. It was a fitting finish to a renascent Joey Dunlop. A meeting only marred by the 250 seizing in practice, it might even have been a clean sweep treble the way he was riding that day; indeed all the fortnight. Retire - never! That was the feeling of several in the paddock.

Not content with an intensive two-weeks racing, the following week saw Dunlop at Dundrod at the '150' chasing Phelim Owens home in the Superkings 125 race with the fastest lap at 103.84mph. In the Regal 600 race, the CBR carried him home in fifth place in a race won by Archibald. Then, back once more at Kirkistown and the man was again banging elbows with the youngsters ending in a mighty scrap with winner of the 1000 race, Michael Swann, and Rodney McCurdy, finishing in that order. The Superbike race was almost a repeat scene, certainly the result was the same, Joey third, and a fastest lap at 93mph.

Anyone who saw Joey overtaking Adrian Archibald at The Skerries by squeezing between him and the bank, almost on the grass, and leaving him to eat the dust thrown up, could hardly doubt that here was a racer who was as determined to win as he ever was. He beat Adrian to win both the big bike races and for good measure grabbed a third in the 125 race. And Archibald was on top form on the day, winning the 600 race.

Joey doesn't miss a race in the Isle of Man, so back for the Southern 100 in July, and he became Southern 100 Champion yet again. It was a privilege to watch him at the start of Wednesday evening's Senior Founders race coming around in fifth place on the RC45 and then pick off the men in front one by one until, getting clear, he simply distanced himself from the field. It left one in no doubt that here was the master of road racing. You'd have thought that it was a man 20 years younger and in his prime of competition life. The Junior event was a field for 125-250-400s. Ian Lougher was the man who put it across the rest of the 250s, while Joey had to fight into second spot after a duel with Richard Coates and Neil Richardson that probably slowed the three of them at its height. Younger brother Robert scooped his bit of glory in winning the 125 class.

Joey got involved in another hectic dice on the Thursday afternoon's programme in the 125s plus 400s event. It was Robert once more taking the win by a wheel from Lougher as Joey came in fourth after dicing hard with Darran Lindsay who shaded third place. The big race of the programme once more saw him storming off into the distance after what seemed a leisurely start but in fact he was lucky even to get to the finish as his rear tyre was already shredding badly. Second place man, New Zealander Blair Degerholm, in the post race interview, said that he needed to get in some gym workouts if he was to challenge Dunlop. 'The Kawasaki takes a bit of holding on to, but I've no excuses, Joey's definitely the boss,' he said.

The 2.6 mile Monaghan circuit on August 15th was the scene of another Lambert & Butler 1st Challenge race. Joey was on the second row with the RC45 against Fireblades and R1 Yamahas and John Donnan scored as Joey came in sixth after skirmishing with Jason Griffiths. The 125 Superkings saw the brothers Dunlop jousting before falling back to ninth in a race won by Owen McNally; a fiercely competitive event in which the lap record was broken by the first three. In the 600 race, no less than six riders broke the lap record as Owen proved his recent form was no fluke by getting out in front. Race two was the real crowd-pleaser as Joey did the business in glorious style taking the Honda UK RC45 to top honours and looked all set to repeat the performance, only to be sidelined by lack of sparks in the 250.

To say that Joey turned the clock back yet again at the Ulster Grand Prix would be trite. The statistics simply record that the legend that is Joey Dunlop chalked up his 48th race on the Dundrod circuit and 24th GP win.

In the first Superbike race, the 1000cc V & M R1 Yamahas of Jefferies and Duffus, had had their day in pushing Joey's 750 into third, though not without Joey forcing into second on several occasions. However, revenge came in the second 'big' race though it should be said that the V & M pairing had a coming together in the 600 race, in which Joey had a good fifth, which took the edge off Duffus. But it was the manner in which Dunlop held off Jefferies' last lap challenge that had the crowd on their feet. David put in a record last lap at over 125mph to come back into striking distance only to be outfoxed by Joey holding the inside line at Wheelers and going wide into the Hairpin. He got the power on early and kept the lead through Quarries to take the chequered linen first.

All this neglects the 125 race which was just as bitterly contested and in fact no less than respected journalist Norrie Whyte, from his considerable experience, described the day's dicing as '110 per cent and not always a good thing on the public roads.' It was Phelim Owens who got home first with Joey second, Ian Lougher third and Gary Dynes fourth. A retirement on the first lap meant that the meeting wasn't all good for Joey. But to put in a race average of over 125mph and against faster, bigger capacity machines, said that the Dunlop legend continued to grow. In fact Honda's Bob McMillan was so pleased with Joey's performance that he gave him the RC45.

The Lambert & Butler event on September 4th at Carrowdore saw Joey take the 250 Payne Honda out against all the bigger bikes to a seventh place. A week later at Killalane on the Saturday, problems on the 250 slowed Joey's progress which meant a third place behind Gary Dynes and winner Darran Lindsay. The Sunday's 125 race saw Dunlop into fourth after fitting new rings and the motor losing its edge. The Harris entered 600 scored him a fourth while the Payne 250 gave him a third place.

The New Millennium beckoned. Joey had had yet another incredible year jousting with the new pretenders and the legend had clearly not lost any of its potency. During the winter of '99, the news began to leak that Joey would tilt once more at Anno Domini with a vee-twin 1000cc.

Phillip McCallen on Joey - quote from Ulster TV.

'He's a multi-world champion, 21 times TT winner and he's never changed. Joey is just Joey.'

The time 6.30am. The year, 1999. Joey had just broken down so there was plenty of time for a cuppa thanks to Deputy Sector Marshall Ian Hunter of Kirk Michael.

R.H.PAYNE

Into 2000 with the vee-twin

his finest hour

At the Irish Motorcycle and Superbike show, Bob McMillan formally presented Joey with the RC45 that would find a home hanging in the roof of Joey's Bar. RC45s officially made their retirement in favour of the vee-twin for Superbike competition, and indeed became Joey's choice for the FI and Senior TT's. The relaxation of the TT FI regulations allowing four cylinder engines up to 1,000cc had handicapped the RC45 (a mere 750cc) and gave the R1 Yamahas a horsepower advantage.

The plan that had served Joey so well in the last two winters, in getting into top fitness for the new season, was again put into place; Australian sunshine was the key. This time, five weeks in OZ worked its familiar magic in deep-healing old injuries. Australia offers not only sunshine, but also anonymity on a free-wheeling motorcycle for the man who had always shunned publicity.

A test session at Darley Moor on the Paul Bird Vimto SP1, and delayed arrival of works engines for the Special Fireblades, made Joey's choice of the vee-twin for his 2000 campaign an easy one. He was reportedly happier with the twin, even though it was a 'kitted' engine and not the full works specification used in the World Superbike Championships. However, it was still good enough to put Joey among the front runners at the North West 200 until a failing rear tyre left him to run home in fifth. But, the new one didn't get that far in the second race, as it too shredded and he actually got the black-flag when the rubber gave up the ghost. There had been a limited choice of 'boots' in the preferred sizes.

Before that though, he had dusted off the winter's rust at Aghadowey by taking the Payne 250 to a couple of second places. The Easter meeting at Aghadowey was something of a family affair. On Saturday, there was a fifth and sixth on the 125 Honda as he beat brother Robert in the second race, while nephew Paul Robinson beat both his uncles with second and third. Joey tested the John Harris 600 in the Regal round for tenth place. Two days later at Kirkistown, he took the 125 to 3rd in the first race and sixth in the second after a three-way dice with Robert and Mark Lunney. The 600 was placed ninth. A week later, the annual Cookstown meeting, run in torrential rain, saw Joey in fine style; finishing second to Darran Lindsay on the 125, followed by a second place on the 250. However, a new

Joey was always a 'hands on' rider and liked to have real input into machinery set up. He is pictured getting involved during a test session at Jurby airfield prior to the 2000 TT.

experience for his long career was to be excluded from that second placing as he had slid of at the Orritor Corner while in the lead as the rubber bar grip came off. He quickly remounted but this is unfortunately not allowed under National regulations. The testing and set up programme for the SP1 continued as a second place from the second wave could only be accounted promising, while in the second Superbike event, fate decided that Joey's Aria visor should mist up to spoil what looked likely to be a win.

That traditional pre-TT meeting, Tandragee, took place on the 20th April. There was a new and very tight chicane brought into use, which did not go down well with many competitors leading to talk of a rider strike. Nevertheless, Joey was on top form taking 1st place on the 125, the only race he contested on the day, though he did complete the sighting lap on the 600.

TT2000 - his finest hour

The TT's capricious weather seemed to be riding on the shoulder of the 48-year-young TT hero and Joey's vast Mountain circuit experience had always enabled him to make inspired judgments on tyres and race strategy. This year was to be no exception. But, before that, the SP1 had given problems in the navigation department as the front end was proving to be somewhat wayward over the bumps and jumps. Bob McMillan, now Honda's Racing Manager UK, was 'on the case' as a swinging arm from Aaron Slight's Superbike found its way onto the SP1. The motor, too, was a World Superbike engine, brought in by HRC to tackle the Yamaha 1000cc fours head-on. While this didn't provide the complete solution the special Dunlop front tyres flown in time for practice halfway through the rain and fog troubled week, made a difference, but experimenting continued. Even so, the bike was still to be seen weaving on parts of the course during the race.

A 118mph lap in practice on the Harris CBR showed Joey's growing confidence in the class as the 250 posed its own problems. Twice he only went as far as Quarter Bridge before returning to the paddock via the back roads for adjustments. The good side of things was that the 125 was actually behaving itself.

As the competitors lined up for the FI race, the weather had been difficult and there were remaining wet patches and swirling clouds that were just lifting over Snaefell. The variable

After a delayed start Joey won the 250 in the 2000 TT; without doubt his favourite class. This was his second win of the week.

conditions were positively made for the Master of the Mountain. From the off, his monumental experience of the course enabled him to skate over the damp patches as David Jefferies and Michael Rutter took a little time to really come to the boil; meanwhile, Joey was escaping from his pursuers. Nevertheless, Jefferies was 'up for the challenge' and gradually speeded up after lap one, to recover time on the second, cracking in a lap at over 122mph, pulling back nine seconds that put him back into contention.

They both took fresh rear rubber at the second lap pit-stop as David continued to eat into Joey's lead. That the Honda twin could go head to head with the R1 Yamaha four was proven by the speed clocked through the Grandstand as Joey recorded an incredible 171mph, a couple of miles-per-hour advantage over the Yamahas. As Dunlop's lead gradually decreased, at the lap four pit-stop the timekeepers actually had Jefferies in front by just half a second. It seemed fitting on the day that while pit-stops have tended to be the Achilles heel of Joey's backup team, on this day it was the pit crew who gave him six seconds advantage as old and new generation of TT riders went for their fourth laps. However, the terrific effort by David Jefferies that had put him in with the chance of snatching victory on the last lap came to nothing as the Yamaha motor cried enough and Joey was away on his own. Rutter was now over a minute in arrears. The crowded grandstand erupted with applause as the living legend wrote victory number 24 into the record books. At the Summerland prize presentation they practically took the roof off in acclamation. Many times has Joey received thunderous applause at the Villa Marina, but this set new records in decibels.

Joey Dunlop declared after the race: 'That was probably one of my best wins. The pressure was on me for that one. With all the Japanese people around here and with Aaron Slight's World Superbike Motor in, it was going to be hard. I struggled on the fast stuff early in practice but I did a lap on Wednesday and I knew we had a chance. By then we'd decided that there was nothing wrong with the chassis.'

Monday's news was of weather again as postponement after postponement was announced. Finally they got away to a 250 race in which the length was reduced to three laps. John McGuinness was expected to be the main challenger, but as always Joey seemed to revel in the conditions and just rode away from the field in a manner that defied superlatives and made a description of the race progress almost irrelevant, given Joey's procession to the flag. Win 25 was almost an anticlimax.

The Manx Government marked win 25 in a very special way. At the prize-giving, one more honour was heaped upon the man from Ballymoney as The Hon. David Cretney, MHK Minister for Tourism and Leisure, presented Joey with a replica of the Manx Sword of State, only the third rider to receive one. Previous recipients were Stanley Woods and Japanese rider Mitsuoh Itoh. Yet another recognition of Joey's phenomenal run of TT wins occurred when, on the Tuesday of race week, he was installed as President of the TT Riders Association. With a shorter-style haircut than one has been used to seeing on the wee man, and an unaccustomed collar and tie for the occasion, he said that he had intended to wait for retirement before accepting. 'But it just doesn't seem to happen, especially while the wins keep coming,' said Joey. Club Secretary Allan Robinson told the crammed meeting, that Joey was not a man for the formalities that attend such AGM's. And with bikes to prepare for Wednesday's race, Joey seemed grateful to leave a meeting concerned with establishing 'The Friends of the TTRA,' a club for supporters and sponsors wishing more involvement in the TT.

Peter Williams, retiring President of the TT Riders Association, congratulates Joey on his appointment as the new President. As a mark of respect, the TTRA decided to leave the position vacant for the remainder of 2000.

As Wednesday's 125 race contenders assembled their machines on the grid, a short postponement was announced while a band of light rain passed across the Island. One could almost hear the muttering in the paddock about 'Dunlop weather' as the conditions conspired in favour of the wee man from Northern Ireland. On the first lap of the race, both Joey and McGuinness chose to pit in order to get in a flying last lap, which also gave them a clear pit lane as the field went through. In spite of his pit-stop, Joey still led on the road and went his merry way to win number 26. There really wasn't much more to say, except that on the day he was in a class of his own, commenting afterwards that in fact 'conditions had been good with no problems' in the race. This was his fifth 125 win.

As Joey pulled into the paddock to tumultuous acclaim from the crowd, he said to commentator Geoff Cannell, speculating on more wins to come that week: 'That he was starting to get a bit tired.' It was quoted as his 96th race start since that memorable event in 1976 when The Maun made his Island debut and the legend was born.

The Junior, 600, race was to follow. Tired or not, Joey went off the line in his usual undramatic style on the John Harris CBR in perfect race conditions and his fourth place in qualifying suggested the possibility of yet another rostrum visit. Fellow Ballymoney resident Adrian Archibald had broken the lap record in practice and looked the 'man most likely to.' But it was Jefferies who led on the first lap by six seconds with a new record, as Joey cracked in his fastest ever lap on a 600; only a couple of seconds outside the existing record, which stood at 18m 53.2s - 119.86mph.

After initial handling problems during the practice week, the Honda vee-twin was to take Joey to his fastest TT lap, at 123,87mph.

Into lap two and there seemed to be little chance of anyone holding David Jefferies as he then went on to close on 121mph for the class. At the pit-stop, Joey was nine seconds behind the flying V & M Yamaha after the refuelling, with team-mate Ian Lougher chasing hard, just a second behind him. Archibald too was motoring, moving into second place and passing Joey on time with a new lap record at over 121.15mph. Lougher then put in his effort to lead Joey by a couple of seconds, which bumped him off the podium. Joey had improved his times in the 600 class and by now all idle talk in the paddock of him retiring had vanished. There was just the Senior race to go now as Joey pulled out of the Production event officially, in any case not having recorded any practice times.

Senior day dawned dull, with slight rain that grew heavier and the talk was of 'Joey weather' yet again as the first race of the day, the Production event, was repeatedly put back. Eventually, some six hours late, it ran as a two-lapper and provided yet another win for David Jefferies, but the Senior was postponed until the Saturday as the dreadful conditions were rightly deemed to be too dangerous to run the big race.

With near dry roads all round on Saturday and Joey starting number six as his fastest qualifying lap speed denoted, the lap record holder, Jim Moodie, was absent from the grid. He had broken with Honda at the last moment, not wanting to ride what he said was an uncompetitive Fireblade. It was David Jefferies who led the field away and at Glen Helen the clock said that Joey's rasping world Superbike vee-twin unit had carried him to equal first place with David's V & M R1 Yamaha; a cracking race was on as Rutter led the charge of the chasing pack.

By Ramsey Hairpin, Jefferies led by seven seconds from Rutter as Joey slotted in two seconds back in third place. First, lap stats indicated David running away with the race with a lap at over 122mph; Rutter was second, 12 seconds down as Joey closed on him to get within 0.9s in third place. On the second run through Glen Helen, Joey had passed Ian Lougher on the road and had clear air in his pursuit of Jefferies, but was now 17 seconds in arrears. However, Rutter too was on the charge and pulled back a couple of seconds at Glen Helen as they raced towards their pit stops for the first time.

Jefferies took fresh rubber and departed before anyone else appeared as Joey also took on a new rear boot, but some were going through to crack in three non-stop laps. This dropped Joey down to fifth with McGuinness and Lougher leap-frogging Yer Maun. At half race distance, it was clearly the day of the V & M Team as Jefferies led team-mate Rutter by 28 seconds while Lougher's gearchange mechanism broke in the pits as he went to restart.

Lap four and Joey was now a minute behind the flying Yorkshireman, and holding onto third place, pit stops and flying laps shuffled the pack again. With his third new tyre of the race fitted, it looked as though only luck could stop Jefferies parading to the flag and the only question seemed to be who would get the places, as Joey and Rutter were dicing together on the roads but separated on time.

The last lap was the only flying one for most competitors and therefore the fastest. In his last lap, Jefferies cracked in a new outright record for the TT course with a time of 18m 0.6s at over 125mph and a 121.95mph race average. He took the chequered flag for his third win of the week, just like Joey. Michael Rutter made second and said he enjoyed his dice with Joey on the roads in which Dunlop clocked his fastest ever TT lap once more, at 123.87mph, to secure third place. The legend rolled on - a triple winner at 48! It didn't seem possible.

As Joey viewed the journey back to Ireland, it would be for a civic reception in his home town of Ballymoney where a hero's welcome was being prepared. Mayor William Logan was to host the reception in his honour at the Town Hall. Meanwhile, the town council of Ballymoney had sent a message of congratulations to The Island after the 25th win, saying: 'It is difficult to compare the standard and comparative difficulty of your many victories, but we think of you particularly as the King of the Isle of Man.' Any one of his 40,000-odd fans on The Island would have agreed.

As a postscript to what Joey saw as one of his best ever wins at the TT, fate then chose to deny us the living legend that was William Joseph Dunlop OBE, MBE. Great friend Andy McMenemy's recent demise was a bitter blow and Joey chose the solace of the 2,000 mile drive to Tallin in Estonia, in preference to his regular Skerries meeting. Here, far from the media, his talents and humility have engendered another huge following for the wee man from Ballymoney. On Sunday, July 2nd, having already won the Superbike and 600 races, Joey slid off the 125 in the wet while leading and crashed into trees surrounding the road circuit. The meeting was abandoned.

I was actually working on this last chapter, nearing the end of five years work, as a phone call from Northern Ireland collaborator Kenneth Boyd, revealed the tragedy. No words of mine could adequately express the immense public upwelling of support and sympathy for Joey's family and eulogies from many that knew him. I shall not try, except that to say, he has left an indelible mark on the world of motorcycle road racing. He must surely be remembered as its greatest modern day exponent and a modest gentleman possessed of great humanity. The King is dead. Long live the Kings of The Mountain.

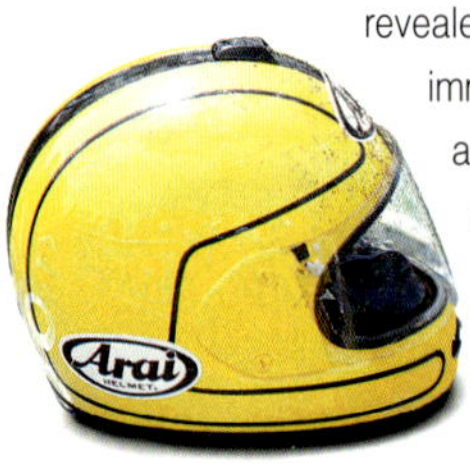

Joey Dunlop must surely be remembered as the greatest modern day exponent of motorcycle road racing and a modest gentleman possessed of great humanity.

About the author

Ray Knight competed for 36 years as a road racer before being hung up by his leathers in the famous Isle of Man Nobles Hospital. He made a debut into racing in 1958 in the MCC High Speed trials riding a Royal Enfield Super Meteor. The Manx Grand Prix followed in 1962 on a home-built Royal Enfield Meteor Minor-powered AJS 7R, the 'Redplum.' That was the first of the 32 years in which he rode the Mountain course, sometimes in both the TT and MGP, totalling 85 times. A Production 500 class TT winner in 1968 aboard a Triumph Daytona, he set lap and race records at over 90mph that would stand for three years.

He was a winner of the 500cc class in the Motorcycle 500 Mile race and 3rd on a Thruxton Bonneville at Brands in the same event, before riding a Laverda Jota into third place in the 10-lap Production TT race. In the intervening years he became a long distance racing devotee on the continent with rides for Norton, BMW and on the Tompkinson BSA at Le Mans. He notched up a class win on a BMW in the Barcelona, Montjuic Park, 24-hours race.

As journalist and race machine tester, he wrote for 30 years on production racing with titles like *Motorcyclist Illustrated, Motorcycle Racer, The Motorcycle and Motorcycle Sport.* Having published five books on racing, he latterly also rode a huge variety of Japanese machinery before retiring after an 'off' on the Isle of Man Jurby South Road circuit in 1994. In racing retirement, he instructs in the local road racing school and restores and parades classic machines and has written for *The Classic Motorcycle, Old Bike Mart, Classic Racer and Classic Bike.*